I Didn't Tell Them ANYTHING

the Wartime Secrets of an American Girl

To Jamie —   5/26/15

Aleena Rieger

[signature]

I Didn't Tell Them Anything: The Wartime Secrets of an American Girl

Map illustrations on pages 36 and 90 by Maureen Burdock.

Published by Sunpetal Books
SunpetalBooks@gmail.com

ISBN: 978-0-9909942-0-6 (paperback)
ISBN: 978-0-9909942-1-3 (EPUB)
ISBN: 978-0-9909942-2-0 (Kindle)
ISBN: 978-0-9909942-3-7 (iOS)
LCCN: 2014919386

For Emma, Summer, Justin, and JP

Contents

Preface .... *vii*

1   Bratislava, 1945 1
2   Mundek—Before 5
3   Kraków, 2002 15
4   Rózia—Before 24
5   September 1, 1939 31
6   Marriage 38
7   The Cattle Cars 44
8   Siberia 48
9   Buying a Train 54
10   Dzhambul 64
11   Our Life in Dzhambul 72
12   Escape 83
13   Poland, 1945 92
14   Borders 95
15   Bratislava, 1945 98
16   The Transom 103
17   Displaced Persons 107
18   Henek Marries Again 116
19   Our Life in Fürth 119

20   Józek   128
21   The Red Scare   133
22   Marine Tiger   138
23   The Golden Land   145
24   My Mother, Rózia—1948   151
25   School   160
26   Becoming an American Girl   167
27   The Names We Had   173
28   Talking About It   178
29   My Mother—After   183
30   My Father—After   186
31   Return to Kazakhstan   192

Acknowledgments   *205*

Preface

IN THE DAYS FOLLOWING the terrorist attacks on the twin towers of New York City on September 11, 2001, impromptu bulletin boards sprang up, on lampposts, tree trunks, and walls, with photographs of men and women, some blond, others dark, often smiling, holding children, but all bearing the same message: "Have you seen...?" "Do you know...?" "Searching for..." Passing one such wall in Grand Central Station, I was suddenly flooded with childhood memories of other makeshift bulletin boards, of hushed conversations, letters, furrowed brows, in the displaced persons camp in Germany where I lived with my parents in postwar Europe. In the weeks after 9/11, as New Yorkers searched for loved ones, I relived those years when my parents and other survivors searched, fruitlessly, for anyone who was still alive, for a life that no longer existed. Then I knew I had to write my parents' story and to uncover and accept, finally and truthfully, my own history.

"Where were you born?" A simple question. But when I was growing up, it was one of four things I wasn't allowed to speak about to outsiders. The other three were my parents' lives before the war, their experiences during the war, and my mother's illness.

My mother and father came from Poland. They were there September 1, 1939, the day the Nazis invaded Poland. The day the second world war began.

My father spoke little about the war years. My mother had little memory and could not speak about them. My family's history was etched in my memory before I knew I had memory. I understood their pain. I tried to shield them and asked no questions. I thought I knew everything. I knew why I couldn't tell the truth about my birth; I knew the reasons our family history had been changed; and I understood that our true history was so complicated, the reasons for prevarication rooted in complex geopolitical situations, that for years I couldn't—and wouldn't—permit myself to even think about the true circumstances of my birth.

And then my grandchildren were born. I wanted to answer their questions about my origins truthfully, but I knew there would be more questions. Nevertheless, I was determined to set my family history— my history—straight. My parents were no longer alive, so telling their story could no longer hurt them. But, because they were no longer alive, I could not ask questions that had been too painful to ask. I had to find the answers myself. Then, in searching for those answers I came across other questions and discovered that I had not known everything.

Sometime after my mother died, my father phoned. He said he had met a writer at the mall where he sat with friends over morning coffee. "I told him a little, you know, about the war. The writer said he wants to write a book about our escape, the journey across Russia to Kazakhstan. But I told him, 'No. My daughter will write our story.'"

"Me?" I spluttered. "I'm not a writer. I don't know enough."

"You know it. You will do it."

I did plan to record his memories. Then my older daughter became engaged and there were wedding plans. I became distracted. My father died a few months after the wedding.

Before my father died, he had reluctantly agreed to be interviewed for a video made by the USC Shoah Foundation Institute for Visual History. He called me the night before his "Shoah video" interview would take place.

"I don't know what to say."

"Just tell the truth. Tell where you were."

"I don't know…"

"What can hurt you now?"

In the Shoah video, he appears pained. He does not seem to hear the interviewer's questions and has to be called back from his reverie with a gentle "Mr. Rieger." He seems confused. When asked by the interviewer about the birth of his daughter—me—he replies, "Can we leave that alone?"

I've thought a lot about my father's reluctance to speak to outsiders about the past, about the pain of loss he suppressed, about the experiences and complete stories he was unwilling to reveal. The father I knew was straightforward and direct, an honest man. During the war, he was forced on many occasions to be less than honest, to fabricate a story, to be someone he was not. He did these things in order to survive, to get across a border, to get to a safe place, to protect his family, to get food for his family. He did what he had to do.

I've thought about the choices people make when it appears they have no choice, the choices my father and mother made. They chose to struggle, to try to get to a better place, to protect me. They chose to attempt dangerous escapes, endure hardships, conceal facts. They chose not to look back at what we had lost, but to look to the future. They chose to try and retain their humanity, their kindness, their sense of humor.

For my grandchildren and those who come after, I will tell my parents' history—and mine—as best as I know it. In doing so, I add my voice to the world's yearning for peace, to the hope for tolerance among peoples, to the wish for an end to wars that affect ordinary persons who want nothing more than to live ordinary lives in ordinary times, with ordinary pleasures, ordinary goals for the future, and ordinary dreams for their children.

1

❦

Bratislava, 1945

M<small>Y EARLIEST MEMORY, WHEN</small> I was three, is of stealing through forests and climbing up and down hills. I'm with a group, my mother, father, and several others. Everyone is very quiet. My father is carrying me on his strong shoulders. I don't like being carried.

"*Tatuś*," I call, "*Sama, sama!*" Father. Myself! My father tries to quiet me, but I am persistent: "*Sama!*" Finally, he lifts me off his shoulders and stands me on the hillside. I climb, proud to be alongside the adults, grabbing small bushes and branches to hoist my way up. I'm almost to the top of a hill when I reach for a shrub that comes out by its roots and I'm hurtled backward, rolling sideways like a log, all the way to the bottom. I howl at the humiliation. I have not proved I'm a big girl. I don't understand the alarm in my father's eyes as he shushes me. "I'm not hurt!" I howl. The adults look around fearfully and at last I stop. My father's strong arms lift me back onto his shoulders and, in that way, we continue.

Later in that journey, another memory. This time we're on a train. I know I'm supposed to use only certain words and not use other words that belonged to the country we had left.

The train stops. Fierce-looking men in brown uniforms come to where we are sitting. They exchange a few words with my father. Then one big man picks me up. His jacket is scratchy and the brim of his cap is too close to my face. "You're a nice little girl," he says in a conversational tone, carrying me out of the train. "*Ponimayit po russki?*" Do you speak Russian? I'm pleased at the compliment but don't answer.

The big soldier carries me out of the train car into a small cabin. Two soldiers stand at attention at each end of the room and two chairs face each other in the middle. He puts me down on one chair and sits opposite.

"What's your name?" he asks in Russian.

I sit still.

"I bet you have a pretty name. Is it Natasha? Maybe it's Anna?"

I sit in silence.

"You must be tired. You've been on the train a long time, haven't you? Where are you from?"

Silence.

"Are you Greek? You can say '*da*' and I'll let you go."

Silence.

"Do you have a doll? I bet you'd like a doll with a pretty blue dress. What do you think?"

My stomach rumbles.

"Ah, I bet you're hungry," my interrogator continues. "I'll have some bread and butter brought in, and maybe some *pieroshki* with *smetana*. I bet you'd like that, wouldn't you?"

Silence.

He takes something out of his pocket. "Would you like an apple?" He reaches out his hand, offering me the succulent treat.

I look at it. My mouth waters. Finally, I open my mouth.

"Mama."

He holds the apple. He continues asking questions, I don't know for how long. I never waver. The only word I utter is "Mama."

At last, the large soldier puts the apple back in his pocket, picks me up, and marches me back to my family. Handing me to my father, he says:

"She doesn't know Russian. You can go."

By my family's reaction I know I have done something important, but I don't know the reason. I only know that I must never say we have been in Russia. I don't care. "I hate that country, and I'm never going to use those words again!" I declare.

In the next few years, it became even more important for my family to keep their years in Russia a secret. But to understand why that was so, and how they got there, I need to go back to the beginning.

Litwo! Ojczyzno moja, ty jestes jak zdrowie,
Ile cie trzeba cenic ten tylko sie dowie,
Kto cie stracil. Dzis pieknosc twa w calej ozdobie
Widze i opisuje, bo tesknie po tobie.

Litwo [Poland]! My country, you are like good health,
How you must be cherished can only be understood
By one who has lost you. Today I see your beauty in its
    entire glory
and I write about it, because I long for you.

from *Pan Tadeusz*
by Adam Mickiewicz
1798–1855

2

Mundek—Before

MY FATHER, MUNDEK, WAS born on June 10, 1912, in Brzostek, a small town near the Tatra Mountains of what is today Poland. At the time, there was no nation called Poland. It had been carved up in the eighteenth century and remained divided until 1918, when my father was six years old.

By 1795 Poland had been divided in three: the Russian czar gobbled the northeast; the Prussian kaiser took the west; and the Austrian emperor grabbed the southeast. The area held by Austria was known as Galicia; it extended south and east from Kraków and included western Ukraine, and its capital was the Ukrainian city of Lwów (called Lemberg by the Austrians and now L'viv by the Russians).

In the eighteenth century, when the province of Galicia was held by Austria, its government treated Jews with tolerance. It's possible that, encouraged by this policy of tolerance, my father's (and my mother's) ancestors migrated to Galicia at that time.

Where would they have come from before they settled in Galicia, these ancestors of mine? Cousin Alan suggests my mother's family came from Spain after the inquisition. Maybe they paused for a few centuries in Prague, where, on a visit, I saw a much-used family name, David Gans, on a headstone in the old Jewish cemetery. My father's family, too, could have come through Prague, the home of a sixteenth-century rabbi with my father's family surname, Judah Loew (another way to spell Löw), famous for creating the mythical story of the dybbuk, a creature who arose from mud to save the Jews from persecution and who, some Jews believed, would rise again in times of trouble. Some of my father's family may have come from other places. His other surname, Rieger, suggests the Latvian city of Riga. It's also possible that one or more of my ancestors came to Polish territory as early as the tenth century, when the first Jews arrived as merchants.

Back to what I know: My father and my mother were born in small towns in the Austrian province of Galicia. By the time they were born, Galicia, and Austria, no longer treated Jews with tolerance. In the nineteenth century, increasingly harsh laws had been passed against Jews, restricting the types of work Jews could do, where they could live, and even how they could marry. Although the government recognized only civil marriages, laws limited the ability of Jews to marry in official civil ceremonies. As a result, most Jews had only religious marriages, not a problem within the Jewish community but an issue when Jews, like my father and his brothers, ventured into the secular world.

When my father enrolled at university (a huge achievement in itself), he was not permitted to use his father's surname, Löw, but was told to use his paternal grandmother's surname, Rieger. When my father protested, the university enrolled him as "Rieger *false* (alias) Löw." By his third year at university, my father gave up and accepted Rieger.

My father grew up in Nowy Sącz (pronounced "Sonch" but called Neu Sandec by the Austrians), a town about one hundred kilometers southeast of Kraków. His father, Izrael Löw, was a career army officer, first in the Austrian army and then, after 1918, in the Polish army. Izrael was a tailor of army uniforms and a furrier; he inspected and labeled furs for the army. After he retired from the army, around 1930, he continued working as a furrier.

Izrael was married twice. With his first wife, he had a son, Albert. After his first wife died, Izrael married eighteen-year old Salamea (Sala or Sara), who raised Albert along with her own three sons: Sine, born in 1910; my father, Mundek, 1912; and Józek, 1914.

Mundek was especially close to his mother. "She was a nice woman, a quiet woman," is all he ever said. Researching the family, I discovered from a distant cousin that her family name was Kuchel and that she was probably the oldest in a large family. Two of her brothers and one sister came to the United States in the 1920s or 1930s, where the family name became Kassell.

Brzostek, Poland, home of my father's grandparents (Sala's parents).

My father said his parents were religious "in the sense that everyone was religious." They lived in a Jewish neighborhood and attended synagogue regularly, "as was expected. It was the way people lived." At home, the family spoke Yiddish and Polish; in the outside world and at school they spoke Polish and German; and the boys also studied Hebrew, the language of prayer. Nowy Sącz boasted a large, beautiful synagogue in the center of town; and smaller *shulelech* or *shtiebel*, places of worship and study or where the *rebbes* lived, dotted the neighborhoods.

My father, Mundek, in round cap in the center, Sine on the left, and Józek on the right, their parents in back.

When Mundek was a boy, in the evenings he often watched his father sew and he learned to mend and make buttonholes. As a teenager, Mundek developed a passion for homing pigeons. He kept them in a coop in his bedroom, trained them, fed them, sent them on "missions," and then watched and waited until they came back to his open window. "He would kiss them on their beaks," a distant cousin remembers.

In Nowy Sącz "we had many organizations," my father said. "Clubs, meetings, social events, sports, chess, dancing, entertainment." He loved sports: soccer, skiing, skating, hiking, swimming in the river. He belonged to the Makkabi football (soccer) club, Tarnowie football club, a chess club, others. As he got older, he went on vacations with his brothers and friends, often to Zakopane in the nearby Tatra Mountains.

"It was a lively Jewish family life. It was a full life. But it all vanished."

℘

In 1978, I visited Nowy Sącz for the first time, with my husband, Richard. My father had not described its beautiful medieval charm. The buildings of Nowy Sącz were preserved because the town had not been bombed by the Nazis during the war, spared because it served as a Gestapo headquarters. We found the bustling *rynek*—the town center—with its Tudor-style town hall. A few blocks north of the rynek, on *ulica* (street) Joselewicza, stood a large, hollow building, the old synagogue, its imposing white stone façade barely visible beneath gray dirt and soot. Built in the eighteenth century, restored after a fire in the late nineteenth century, the synagogue had been renowned for its beautiful baroque façade. During the war, the Gestapo used the building for storage.

When I later visited, in 2008, the synagogue was less gray, now used as a museum and Jewish historical center. I learned that the Jewish community had been composed of two groups: a relatively assimilated population, to which my father's family belonged, and a mystical Hassidic group. Nowy Sącz was the home of a revered teacher, Chaim Halberstam, whose restored grave in the Jewish cemetery on ulica Rybacka just outside the town walls, has once again become a much-visited Hassidic shrine.

℘

My father would not go to Poland, he would not revisit those memories, but before I traveled there the first time, he drew a small map so I could find the street where he had lived, his house, his school. We found the building in which my father grew up, at 22 ulica Grodzka. It was a two-story brick building holding several apartments on a street lined with many similar buildings. We also found the *gimnazjum* (high school) on ulica Jana Długosza, a large brick building several blocks from his home. The buildings were there, bricks and mortar; but the world my father had inhabited no longer existed. Ten thousand Jews had lived there, about one-third of the town's population, but none remained in Nowy Sącz after the war.

In gimnazjum my father studied humanities. "Few Jewish students were able to attend gimnazjum, maybe four or five per class," he said. A quota, called *numerus clausus*, applied to Jewish students in all of Poland. A limited number could attend school. "If someone broke through, once in school, if he was good, they had respect for him. If he was a good student, the teacher liked him and sat him in front." I picture my father, alert, easily liked, sitting in front.

Another reason many Jews were kept from education was because gimnazjum was expensive. Also, there were classes on Saturday, which observant Jews could not attend. "Once in school, as a Jew, you had to be very careful," my father said. "When the school had Christian religious prayers, we had to leave the building, we couldn't even stay in the corridor. So, for several hours we would hang around outside, and then go back in."

It was even harder to attend university. Under the *numerus clausus*, only a very few Jewish students were accepted. Some schools had a *numerus nullus*: no Jews could attend. In many cases, in medical or dental school, only one or two Jews were permitted in a class, and thousands competed.

Mundek wanted to become a doctor. The family thought he had a chance. Izrael, his father, was an officer in the Polish army. "He had many connections," Mundek said. "He was sure that, with my academic record, he could find a way to get me into medical studies. But I was not accepted."

After Mundek was turned down, the family decided he should apply for law and try for medical school the following year. He applied and was accepted into law studies at Jagiellonian University in Kraków. That in itself was a major achievement for a Jew. But it was not what Mundek wanted. He wanted to be a doctor.

My father was twenty years old when he went to the University in Kraków and moved into a Jewish student dormitory at 3 ulica Przemyska where most of the Jewish students lived. On my visit to Poland, I found the dormitory, a gray stone building about a fifteen-minute walk from the law school. I pushed open the heavy wooden door, walked up the ornate staircase to the small sleeping quarters on the upper floors, and imagined my father and his brothers in that building, focused on young men's issues: education, career, meeting girls.

My father was alert and quick but he did not apply himself to law school. During his first year, he was waiting until he could apply again for medicine. The following year he did apply, but was turned down a second time. Once again, during his second year of law school, he again marked time, and then tried a third time for medical school. It was no different. Finally, he accepted that he would not become a doctor. In his third year, he turned more seriously to his law studies but he had to repeat a few courses.

"My family learned its lesson," Mundek said. "My younger brother, Józek, started at Jagiellonian University, studying chemistry and philosophy, and also applied for medical studies, but, like me, was not accepted. So our father sent Józek to medical school in France." Józek was sent to live with their older half-brother, Albert, in Paris. By that time, Albert was a designer of men's evening clothes and had a wife and daughter.

The year was 1936. Mundek was at last determined to become a lawyer. But his father became sick and died quickly. There was less money, and Mundek had to find work to pay for his expenses and school fees, and to help with his mother's living expenses. While continuing his studies in Kraków, he took a part-time job as a clerk in a factory in a nearby town and also commuted to Nowy Sącz to help his mother.

That year also marked a change in the atmosphere in Poland. Anti-Semitism, always present, now developed in a more violent direction. A right-wing anti-Semitic party, whose members were called Endeks, gained prominence. Bands of Endeks roamed the areas of the university.

"They formed gangs at the entrance to the law school," my father said. "They locked the doors and they would not let one Jewish student in. They attacked us, they hit us with whatever they had. We had to step aside; we had to go back to our dormitories.

"They didn't want to educate Jews, they didn't want Jews at all."

Endek came from the initials ND short for Narodna Demokracizja, National Democratic Party, whose slogan was "Poland for Poles." The Endeks did not consider Jews, even those whose families had lived in Poland for five hundred years, as Polish. After 1935, the government in Poland sanctioned and encouraged violence against Jews, encouraging the Endeks and others. Violence erupted throughout Poland as well as on the university campus in Kraków.

There was one especially bad time my father spoke about on the Shoah video:

I was walking to the law school. It was an important day for me. But the entrance to the school was blocked by a violent mob attacking Jews. When we saw what was happening we turned around and ran back to our dormitory, but the mob followed us. "We're going to kill you," they shouted.

When we got to the dormitory, we called the police for help, but the police were slow in responding. In the meantime, we defended ourselves any way we could. We used our metal bed frames to block the entrance to the dormitory. The mob got in anyway. We broke off metal rails from the stair railing to use as clubs, and beat back the rioters as they came up after us.

The police came too late.

Gaudeamus igitur
Juvenes dum sumus;
Post jucundam juventutem,
Post molestam senectutem
Nos habebit humus!

Let us rejoice
While we are young;
After youth's joys,
After old age's melancholy
We shall become the earth.

Latin, thirteenth-century,
university student song

3

Kraków, 2002

"THE POLICE CAME TOO late." My father's voice breaks, uncharacteristically

Too late for what? By the time I hear my father's words on the Shoah video, he is no longer alive. I can't ask him.

My father's past is especially real to me, as though it were my own. I knew my father never got his law degree although he had finished law studies. I accepted his explanation that there were no records, "the war," without question. I didn't ask for details because I understood some things were too painful to be talked about, even to me.

I travel to Poland, to Jagiellonian University, searching for clues. By the time of this, my second trip to Poland, the country has overthrown the Soviet yoke and documents are becoming available.

I've walked the campus and asked directions. At last, I push through a heavy oak door. "*Dzień dobry*," I say in my best Polish. "Good day. Is this the archives department?"

"*Dobry dzień, tak.*" Good day, yes, replies the librarian closest to the door. He looks up at the two well-dressed Americans: me, pale and anxious; my husband, Richard, solicitously at my side.

"I'm searching for my father's records. He studied law here many years ago."

"Oh?" the librarian says, his face impassive. "Before or after?"

"Before," I respond. "In the '30s."

"Your father's name?"

I hesitate. "I'm not sure." Two other librarians, both women and the only other people in the room, look up, curious. How to explain the confusion about my father's last name? What would he have used?

"Rieger," I finally say.

"And his first name?"

Again I pause. "I'm not sure which name he would have used. In the US he was Murray; my mother called him Mundek."

"Edmund," one of the women suggests.

"No, he was never Edmund. He also had a Jewish name. Maybe he used that."

The librarians are in their forties, too young for firsthand memories of the war. The three of them huddle and nod, and the man disappears through a doorway. The two women turn to huge reference books set up on cabinets around the room.

Richard and I remain standing. Why am I here, I ask myself, echoing what my father might have said. It's the past, you can't change it, let it go.

I know I can't change things for you, I say silently to my father's memory, but I need to do this for me, for my children and grandchildren. We have no records, no photos, no stories, even, from before the war. It's as if nothing before me existed.

I look around the cavernous room lined with massive bookshelves filled with worn leather-bound books. Four long mahogany tables and benches fill the dark center of the room. A dusty, ancient globe sits in the far corner. Jagiellonian University is one of the oldest universities in Eastern Europe, founded in 1364. The university museum displays artifacts going back to before Copernicus, an illustrious early alumnus. Newspapers describe the school days of Karol Wojtyla, who became Pope John Paul II and attended the university about the same time my father was there. Surely, I think, if there are records of one student from the 1930s, there's a chance my father's records still exist.

I hear the faint rustle of paper, an occasional murmur from the remaining librarians, and the slow, methodical ticking of an old clock. After an interminable time, the back door opens and the man returns carrying a heavy leather-bound book, which he places on the counter before me. "This may be something," he says.

The year "1936" is stamped in black on the book's spine. The librarian opens it and I look at the page where he holds his fingers. It takes me a while to adjust to the Polish letters, some printed on the form and some in handwritten script. I focus on the name "Rieger."

"Yes," I say, "that's the name." I read further. "It says S-i-n-e. Oh, my god, that's his brother."

Sine. An uncle I never met. My father told me only that his older brother vanished. I try to remember what else my father said about Sine but my thoughts are interrupted by the librarian, who turns to another page: "Look, here's another Rieger."

The handwriting jumps out at me. "*Tak!*" Yes, yes, yes! I shout. "That's him. That's my father."

"Rieger," I read, then "Mojżesz Samuel," surprised that he used his Jewish name. When I was growing up, my father referred to his Jewish name only on official occasions: at my wedding and when my mother died. The document in front of me is my father's enrollment records for the 1935–1936 school year. I force my eyes to focus; I will myself to concentrate on the page. Here at last is a tangible link to my family's history. The stories are not just family legends. They are true.

The three librarians look intently at the book, then talk all at once.

"There may be other years."

"There must be course records."

"I'll research the *Książke Magistrum*," a book that lists all law graduates, they tell me.

"Oh, he wouldn't be listed there," I say slowly, feeling my father's disappointment. "My father couldn't finish his degree."

With energy, the librarians get to work. As the day passes, they bring in bits and pieces of my father's university life: records of enrollment at the start of each year; a list of courses he took, and even a record for another brother, Józek, two years younger than my father.

At the end of the day, I turn to the librarians, who have stayed long past their workday.

"*Dziękuję*," I say.

"No need to thank. *My jesteśmy zadowoleni żmorzemy pomóc.*" They're happy they could help. "We have the satisfaction of having found something important."

The man bows slightly. The women nod and dab at their eyes. I want to hug them, cry, and laugh. Instead, I shake their hands with my own trembling one, clasp copies of the records to my chest, and turn to leave. Behind me, the late afternoon sun casts an amber glow on the burnished tables, the shiny globe. I push the thick oak door and walk out into the bright courtyard, Richard behind me.

We walk through the university's archways and quadrangles, the old and still older buildings, until we find the law faculty. It's a U-shaped, three-story structure of dingy stone surrounding a bare courtyard. Students are emerging through double doors at its center, walking alone or in twos, carrying books, some running, others moving slowly. Nearby, I see the green expanse of *planty*, the promenade of greenery that encircles the old town and the university. In medieval times it was the site of a moat and wall that encircled and protected Kraków.

As Richard and I walk down a path lined by mulberry bushes and leafy oak trees, I imagine my father here: a slender young man with a serious face, hairline already receding, intelligent eyes behind dark rimmed glasses, sensitive mouth and small, strong chin. What did he think as he crossed the planty? Was he alone, deep in thought, or in animated conversation with his brother, or rushing to meet some friends for a soccer game before dinner? As events unfolded, did he become more serious, more careful? On a day like this, at least in his early years, did he sit on a bench in the planty reading a textbook?

In my hands are the records of what he studied, courses not much different from those offered at NYU Law School where I attended: Principles of Political Economy, Constitutional Developments in France since the Revolution, Law of the Nations and Law of Peace, History of Liberalism, Church Law.

Latin epigrams are engraved on the walls of many of the university buildings. I read them aloud to Richard as we walk, and think about the classical education my father had. He encouraged me, too, to study Latin, a "good base for other languages," he said. When my father was in his eighties, we were chatting on the telephone and I mentioned a popular movie of the day which featured the main character, a philosophy teacher, exhorting his students with the Latin "*carpe diem.*" My father recited the entire phrase: "*Carpe diem, quam minimum credula postero.*" Seize the day and don't think about the future.

"But I much prefer '*Quidquid agis, prudenter agas, et respice finem,*" he said. Whatever you do, do it well, and remember your purpose. So much like my father.

On this day, leaving the planty and the University buildings, Richard and I enter the rynek, the old town center which is, in fact, a vast rectangle dominated by a long arcaded building, the Sukiennice or cloth hall. This was a center of fabric and cloth trade in medieval times. Now gift shops and restaurants line the building's arcades and perimeters. The rynek is not much changed from my father's day. As I imagine the clip-clop of horse-drawn carriages on cobblestone streets, I now see horse-drawn carriages ferrying tourists, the sound of their horseshoes muffled on asphalt.

The old town center is teeming with people, pulsing with energy. Shop windows brandish posters, red and black letters advertising toys, souvenirs, vodka, food. Flower stalls are bursting with yellow daffodils, red roses, pink and purple tulips. People walk past, pause to look, to read, their faces interested, their cheeks and lips rosy.

We stop at a toy shop inside the Sukiennice. I watch a pale blond boy of five admiring the wooden toys, pointing to a happy marionette with a long nose and loose limbs. The matronly shopkeeper calls the boy's attention to a carved duck; she sets its splayed feet on an inclined board, and the duck waddles down. The boy laughs and claps his hands. As the boy's mother bargains with the shopkeeper, we hear a violin being tuned. A quartet is arranging an impromptu concert at the corner of the Sukiennice. All around the rynek, artists have set up displays, some with easels.

I'm charmed by this cultural city. My father didn't describe it but I see traces of him everywhere: his love of music, his old-world demeanor, his worldview. The rousing melody of a nearby bugle reminds us that this is a city constantly aware of its history. The *hejnal's* call of alarm ends abruptly, the way it did the night an invader's arrow pierced the neck of the thirteenth-century bugler warning the city's inhabitants of impending attack, the way it does every hour from the tower of St. Mary's Church in this old city.

The structure of the rynek has been the same for more than seven hundred years. The city was not bombed during World War II, unlike most other cities of Poland, so the old town is much like it was when my father went to university. Its medieval architecture is intact. In the distance we see Wawel Hill, upon which stands Wawel Castle, the home of Poland's kings. Its presence dominates the area.

At the edge of the rynek, we come upon an ivy-covered, ancient-looking restaurant with an inviting terrace rimmed by pink and red roses. The menu is full of foods my father loved: pierogi, steaming dough pockets filled with sweet wild berries and topped with rich sour cream, mushroom barley soup with an earthy aroma. Richard and I share fresh rye bread and creamy butter, and finish with yeasty sweet *babka*, redolent with cinnamon and cream. I feel my father sitting next to me, sipping his favorite soup, breaking bread. "This was my city," he might say. "I loved the music, the culture. I had many friends."

Later that evening, Richard and I attend a reception in the home of the US Consul General, a two-story building with glass doors leading to a garden in the back. The reception is on the first floor, the

main rooms comfortably but modestly furnished with beige uphol-
stered couches and chairs. The table is spread with an assortment of
appetizers: canapés with mushrooms, beets, cabbage, potato pancakes
with sour cream. Waiters in black suits and white shirts cross the
polished wood floors carrying trays with glasses of vodka and wine.
The guests themselves are a mix of business executives, university professors, and others who live in the city. I quickly become popular
because I'm one of the few American businesswomen attending who
speak Polish.

I mention I've spent the day searching for my father's records.
Coincidentally, the vice-rector of Jagiellonian University, Professor
Doctor Maria Nowakowska, is at the reception and someone intro-
duces her to me. She is an amiable, intelligent woman with short
brown hair and a noticeable harelip, but a ready smile. After relating
my search and the papers I found earlier that day, and given courage
by the festive surroundings, I ask a newly formed question: "Would
it be possible for the university to grant my father a degree post-
humously? Perhaps the circumstances, the war, could be taken into
account?"

Professor Nowakowska promises to look into it. Several weeks
later, back in my office in New York City, I receive an e-mail. She
informs me that she has done some research of her own, and con-
cludes as follows:

> The Polish name of your father was Mojżesz Samuel Rieger.
> He studied at the Faculty of Law and Administration of the
> Jagiellonian University in the years 1932/33–1936/37. On
> March 17, 1938, he took his final exam, but the result was
> not satisfactory. This was a unanimous decision of the exami-
> nation commission. He was, then, allowed to retake the exam,
> but according to the document he has not done it....
>
> I am afraid that we shall never be able to establish what
> had prevented your father from taking the exam. It is very
> unfortunate for me to have to tell you that I am not autho-

rized to change the decision of the examination commission and grant your father with the magistrum title. It would be breaking the Polish law if I did.

The answer surprises me. My father was too intelligent. The man I knew wouldn't fail. Why did the records show he failed? Could it have something to do with the police coming too late?

I turn my father's words over in my mind. I listen again to his video. Too late for what? I ponder Professor Nowakowska's letter. She said March 17, 1938. My father's final exam result was not satisfactory. Could that be the day? He had to turn back. He never took the exam. The Endeks prevented it. He never retook it. Continued violence prevented it. But he kept trying.

My father was still in Kraków hoping to take his final exam on September 1, 1939.

Mundek, about 1937.

A Yiddishe Momme, nisht du kein besser in der welt.
A Yiddishe Momme, oy vey tzis bisser ven sie fehlt,
Vie shayn und lichtig tzis in hois ven die mama's du,
Vie traurig finster tzvert ven Gott nehmt ihr oyf Oylam habu.
In vasser und fayer volt sie geloif'n fahr ihr kind,
Nisht halt'n ihr tayer, dos iz gevis der greste zind.
Oye vie gliklach und raych is der mench vu hot
Az a tayere matune geschenkt fun Gott,
Wie an altechke Yiddishe Momme, Momme, oy Momme mein.

A Yiddish Mamma, there is no finer in the world,
A Yiddish Mamma, oh it's bitter when she's ill,
How pretty and bright is the house when mama's there,
How sad and dark when God takes her to the other side.
In water and fire would she run for her child,
Not holding her dear, that was the greatest sin.
Oh how lucky and peaceful is the person who has
As a dear guardian sent by God,
Such an old-fashioned Yiddish Mamma, Mamma, oh Mamma mine.

"My Yiddishe Momme," by
Jack Yellen and Lew Pollack,
1925

4

꽃ᛝᛝ꽃

Rózia—Before

WHEN I WAS GROWING up, my mother lost most of her memory. After my parents died, I realized how much I didn't know about her early life. Not many were alive to answer my questions. Distant American cousins sent versions of our family tree, all incomplete and inaccurate. Web research yielded a few clues: I found a history of Jasło, where my mother grew up, and a reference to Izrael Gans, my mother's father, who, coincidentally, had the same first name as my father's father.

I piece together what I know about my mother's early years.

My mother's mother was Debora Ferziger from a well-to-do family of merchants in the small city of Dębica, not far from Jasło. Debora was the youngest child of Chana Shaindel, whose name was given to me as my Hebrew name, and Leibe Ferziger. Chana Shaindel was Leibe's second wife. Their oldest child was a boy, Rubin; Debora had a fraternal twin who did not survive; and there were two sisters. Leibe Ferziger operated an import-export business in the 1880s and frequently traveled to the United States on business. He thought life would be better in the United States and the family immigrated around 1890, a few years after Debora was born.

According to family lore, life in the United States disappointed

Chana Shaindel, who disliked the falling away from a religious life and Jews working on the Sabbath. Two years after they arrived, Chana Shaindel convinced her husband to return to Galicia with their children. But the eldest, Rubin, then twelve, did not want to leave the United States and ran away. They had to board ship without him.

My grandmother Debora was brought back to the small city of Jasło in Galicia at the age of five. According to a surviving elderly cousin, Debora had never learned English and did not remember the United States but, when she became of marriageable age, the matchmaker told the family that, to religious families, Debora had been tainted by her two years in America. A suitable marriage would be difficult.

The matchmaker found Izrael Gans, one of eight children from a family of humble background. I had heard he was a man who could make friends wherever he went, outgoing and boisterous, not intellectual or deep thinking. He worked as a housepainter. On the website about Jasło, I now learn that Izrael Gans was a member of the Zionist movement and was elected to the community board on the workshop owners ticket. The anonymous writer states: "Often he abandoned his business in order to tend to municipal or communal affairs or parliamentary elections. During these activities he was full of anger and fury and defended the rights of the workshop owners and workers to the best of his ability."

On the web, I also find a reference to Izrael's father, Aaron David Gans who owned the only Jewish fish store in town, by the river under the Ulaszowice Bridge. "He was a pleasant person and tried to satisfy his customers."

Only the website, and not a living person, is a link to my ancestors.

彰

Debora and Izrael had four children: Henek, born in 1908; Ita in 1912; my mother on May 28, 1914; and Tulek, born less than eleven months later in April of 1915.

Wedding photo of my mother's parents, Debora and Izrael.

When I visited Jasło in 1978, it was impossible to see what the town had been like before the war. Jasło's entire Jewish population, three thousand persons, one-quarter of the town, had been murdered. Everything had been bombed and, after the war when Poland was controlled by the Soviet Union, rebuilt in the Communist style, with no historic remnants.

The city was shattered and then rebuilt, but never again the same. Like my mother.

❧

In my quest for information about my mother's early years, I searched out my mother's cousin Helen, then in her nineties and failing. She was one of the few people with whom my mother felt comfortable, here in the US. Helen was not willing to share much of her own painful past, but I was content to let her talk in generalities about life in Jasło and whatever she could remember about my mother.

Before the war, Helen said, most of the buildings in Jasło were one- or two-story houses with small gardens, some with a plum or apple tree. Three rivers meandered nearby. Fish was a staple, fried, cooked, or gefilte. On Fridays or holidays, people had soup, often chicken noodle.

My mother's family maintained a kosher home, ate only kosher foods, separated milk dishes from meat dishes, and used separate plates and pots for Passover foods. But Debora, an observant Jew, had a peculiar belief that ham had health-giving qualities. Whenever any of the children became sick, Debora went to the gentile part of town and bought cooked ham. The children were not allowed to tell anyone. Later, when I was growing up, my mother would not eat most foods forbidden to Jews, no bacon or shellfish, but she always ate ham.

In Jasło, my mother's family lived in a small house a few blocks from the rynek. The town was small enough that people walked everywhere. A long street, Kościuszki ulica, led from the rynek to the train station, about two kilometers away. Another street, ulica Czesza Maia, led to a big park. A large and ornate synagogue stood on a hill, and around town rabbis had *shtiebel*, places for study and daily prayer. Everybody in the Jewish community knew everybody else, or at least their families. Every Friday, Jasło held a fair; farmers brought their produce and many people from surrounding villages came.

At the start of the first world war, Izrael was conscripted into a Polish division of the Austrian army. Desperate to get out, he and a friend, concocted a plan. They swallowed chewing tobacco. Whether from the tobacco, as the family always thought, or from something else, Izrael really became ill. He was released from the military with an enlarged heart and other problems. He returned to his wife and children unable to work; he couldn't breathe; he couldn't sleep. The four small children, Henek, Rózia, Ita, and Tulek, took turns staying awake at night next to their father's bed, watching over him.

During the day, Rózia followed her older sister, Ita, everywhere. Their mother had little time for Rózia because she was busy with

Tulek, a hyperactive little boy who was always getting sick. Ita, just two years older than Rózia, took over Rózia's care.

Rózia was energetic. She loved action. "We swam in the river," my mother said, one of her few memories. "We used our slips as bathing suits, pinning them with a safety pin between the legs."

And my mother loved to tell of a time she and a friend scrambled over a neighbor's fence to climb an apple tree. Suddenly, the owner appeared. "He said he would teach us a lesson and give us something to tell our mothers. He made us take off our dresses and leave them so we would have to go home in our slips and explain to our mothers what happened. You should have seen my mother's face!"

My mother's laugh made her sound, for a moment, like a mischievous young girl. She ended with: "My sister always defended me."

My mother's sister, Ita, was the opposite of my mother, a quiet and gentle young woman who stayed home and helped with household chores. She liked to cook and sew, knit and crochet; she made beautiful lace curtains and bedspreads. When she grew older, she never went to work, but she was an active Zionist.

Their father, Izrael, died when my mother was a teenager. Debora's well-to-do uncles and other relatives supported the family. Henek and Tulek went to work as soon as they could.

Tulek moved into an apartment with two friends and the three took over Izrael's painting business. Tulek was soon earning enough to help support the family. Tulek was "a bit on the wild side, but a good boy, a good heart," elderly cousin Helen told me. He looked like his father, already balding as a young man. Like his father, Tulek was charming and made friends wherever he went, but he was also boisterous and outgoing, impatient and quick to erupt in anger. "Ach, he was difficult to live with," my mother always said, but she was fiercely loyal to him and always felt responsible for her brothers.

Henek, the older brother, was quieter in temperament. He was good-looking, with a full mouth and those large eyes, topped by thick dark hair. He went to work for a printer in Kraków and, after a few years, started his own business. He married his childhood sweetheart,

Irana Weiss, and their son, also named Izrael but nicknamed Iziu, was born in July of 1935.

My mother had the most schooling of the siblings. She completed elementary school and, because she was pragmatic and excelled at math, she then attended *handlowa*, a business school. After completing her degree, she worked as a bookkeeper at a company that manufactured and exported shoes, overshoes, and galoshes. The company was owned by Debora's relatives, Aaron Mendel Darr and his brother-in-law Wurtzel, in the town of Krosno, about thirty kilometers from Jasło. Rózia commuted by train every day. In a few short years, she became the head bookkeeper.

Rózia, about 1937.

My mother and father met in 1936. One day, Mundek and his friends rode their bikes from Nowy Sącz to Jasło, where they met up with other friends who lived there, including my mother's sister, Ita. As the friends stood chatting, bikes thrown in the grass, my mother, Rózia, happened by on her bike.

Rózia was headstrong and fiery, two years younger than Mundek. I can picture her riding up to the group, dark bobbed hair framing her face, large eyes flashing with impatience, words tumbling out of her mouth as she spotted her sister.

Mundek and Rózia quickly became a couple. Rózia helped Mundek obtain a part-time job as a law clerk at the business concern where she worked. He was also planning a business venture with a friend and was enthusiastic about starting. All he had to do was take that final exam and get his law degree from the university.

☙

"Your mother introduced me to your father in 1938," cousin Helen says. "I had a summer job in Żegiestów, near Krynica, a resort area. I played the piano with a small band in a restaurant. Your mother and father came in to dance."

"What were they doing in Żegiestów?" I am surprised at this vision of my parents, young and dancing.

"They came on vacation. They were engaged to be married. Rózia looked for me to show off her fella. We spent some time together for the next two weeks. We had a good time, canoeing and swimming. They were very much in love."

☙

On September 1, 1939, Rózia was in Jasło making preparations for her wedding, waiting for Mundek, who was to arrive by afternoon train from Kraków.

5

September 1, 1939

Mundek woke on September 1, 1939, in his dormitory in Kraków to hear on the radio and in the streets that the Nazis had invaded Poland. "The Nazis were killing Jews on the street, in their homes, everywhere," my father said.

"So we ran. Wherever. However."

Mundek quickly filled a rucksack with a few precious possessions. Thinking back on hints and comments he made over the years, I have come to believe that one of these possessions was a document showing that he had, at last, completed all steps required for his law degree; the document had yet to be entered in the records department at the university.

He and a friend jumped on their bicycles and pedaled rapidly down the road, away from the advancing Nazi military might. East.

"Bombs rained over our heads. We saw hell on earth."

They lost all sense of time. They lost all sense of direction.

On their second or third day, they saw an apple orchard. Not having eaten for days, they fell on the apples, devouring as many as they could, all the time keeping an eye on the sky for the murderous Stukas.

Too many apples made them sick. But they couldn't stop. They continued on their bikes. Most of the time, they rode in the dark of night and slept during the day in deep grasses where they buried their bikes.

"We went until there was no hiding place."

My father could have heard on the radio, days before the Nazi attack, that on August 23, 1939, Nazi Germany and the Soviet Union had signed a nonaggression treaty which stated that the Soviet Union would not intervene if Germany invaded Poland. But there was a secret protocol to the treaty that my father would not have known about. Under this secret protocol, which became known only after the war ended, the two countries agreed to divide Poland in half at the Bug River. Nazi Germany would take the portion west of the river and the Soviet Union would take the eastern portion, which included western Ukraine.

As a result of this secret protocol, on September 17, a bit more than two weeks after the Nazis attacked Poland from the west, the Soviets entered Ukraine and Poland from the east.

Mundek and his friend frantically pedaled from west to east as the Nazi blitz advanced on their heels, in a direction that took them toward the Ukrainian city of Lwów. They were fleeing the fire but didn't know they were jumping into a white hot frying pan.

They staggered into Lwów. By the time they got there, the Nazis had already reached that city but, because of the secret protocol, were retreating as the Soviets came in from the east.

"In Lwów, the streets, the houses were shattered. Dead horses. Dead people. Everywhere. We had nowhere to go. We searched for friends, a place to hide, but there were no hiding places."

Mundek and his friend decided their bikes were a danger: "They would think we were the Polish army, coming on bikes." So they threw their bikes into the river. Then they had to walk.

And, somewhere along the way, my father and his friend became separated. "I didn't know where he went." My father never saw this friend again.

❦

In Lwów, my father looked for a place to stay, for something to eat. He remembered that my mother's cousin Helen, the one who played the piano when they were courting, had moved to Lwów several years earlier. He said: "I found Helen's apartment. I knocked on the door. From the other side, she called out. She heard me. But she would not let me in."

Some moments in life are indelible. This incident of refusal my father told only to me. In later years, in the US, my mother remained friends with Helen all her life. My father was polite but avoided visiting Helen. He never told my mother about the incident in Lwów.

What kept Helen from opening that door? Clearly, she was afraid. The Soviets kept a tight watch. During this time in the early part of the war, when the Soviets were allied with the Nazis, the Soviets considered Poland as the enemy, and the persons flocking from western Poland to eastern areas were perceived as the enemy. The Soviets would have dealt harshly with locals harboring the enemy. Still, many people opened their doors to the refugees from the west and took that chance. Why are some people brave and others not? Can I blame Helen for her fear? How would I have reacted?

As for my father, he kept fleeing: "I made it to Podwołoczysk, but the Nazis took it over, then the Russians. It was impossible. For us, both were dangerous. Everything was falling apart. Everyone was killing Jews: Nazis on one side, Russians on the other. We had no place to go, but I had to keep running, keep hiding."

≈

In the meantime, on September 1, 1939, my mother was in Jasło with her mother and her brothers, dreaming of the wedding, waiting for Mundek. She knew how reliable he was. But, early in the day, news came to Jasło that the Nazis had invaded Poland. Everyone, especially the Jews, feared the consequences and rushed to find a safer place.

Henek, with his wife and son, had left his home in Kraków and arrived in Jasło at the end of August, searching for a place the Nazis would not invade, as had been rumored. But after September 1, they knew even that small town was not safe. People believed men were in the most danger and Henek's wife urged him to leave town. Reluctantly, he separated from Irana and Iziu, only for a short time he thought, and he, too, fled east. Nazi bombers attacked the train Henek was on. He jumped off and ran. "Two Stukas dove in," he later said. "The men on either side of me dropped. I kept going."

❧

My mother's three young cousins, Oskar, eight, David, eleven, and Selma, thirteen, had also come to Jasło at the end of August, brought there by their mother after the family was forced to leave their home in Düsseldorf, Germany. Their father, Sam Gans, had roots in Jasło, but he was not with them; he was in America trying, unsuccessfully, to arrange passage for his family. When it became clear that Jasło would not be safe, the children's mother traveled to her hometown, Buczacz, in north-central Poland to seek a safer place. From there, she dispatched a telegram: "Send the children."

Tulek quickly escorted the three to the train station. As Tulek put the children on the train, he still hoped theirs would be an ordinary journey. He spoke to the conductor: "Watch out for their luggage, don't let it get lost."

Later, Tulek himself squeezed onto a train going east.

❧

My mother, Rózia, remained with her sister, Ita, and their mother, Debora. After a few days, the women realized their lives, too, were in danger.

"Ita and I talked," my mother told me as small fragments of memory surfaced in her later years. "Our mother was not strong enough to run. Ita told me to leave; she would stay. I refused. I wanted the three of us to be together. But Ita said I should go and find Mundek; he would need me." With that argument, my mother finally agreed to go. But she was plagued by her decision all her life, even before memory began to come back. "I had a sister once," she'd say over and over, as if telling me for the first time, as if she could have saved Ita had she stayed.

When Rózia fled Jasło, she put a change of clothes and a few pieces of bread into a small sack and followed the throng of people going east. For a while, she rode on someone's wagon, but then the people split up for safety; they thought they were too visible to the airplanes overhead and would be a target for the bombs. "Most of the time I walked," she said. "I didn't know where I was going. I just knew I couldn't stop."

On one day of walking, Rózia was confronted by a Nazi soldier.

"Where do you think you're going? You! Jew!" he demanded, raising something over her head, a club or a rifle, she never knew.

"*Matka Boska*"—Mother of God—Rózia protested, "I'm not a Jew, I'm not!" She showed me how she had crossed herself in the way of her Catholic friends, and she recited a prayer she'd heard them say. But even as she "prayed," the soldier brought his club down on her head, and beat her unconscious. Maybe that was the first cause of her later lost mind.

≈

Tulek reached Lwów, and found Helen's apartment. Henek arrived soon after. They left after a few days, knowing it was too dangerous for Jews to be together. When my father arrived at Helen's about a week later, he did not know that Tulek and Henek had already been there.

They all had to keep moving. Jews together were a target for Nazis, for Soviets, for Ukrainians.

Tulek and Henek walked for four days, 150 kilometers further east to the city of Tarnopol.

Somehow, my mother also made her way to Tarnopol. Somehow, Henek and Tulek found her.

≈

My father, too, ran east from Lwów to Tarnopol. There, my father sought out the Jewish community. People opened their homes and gave food and shelter to the refugees. Then, one day, in the rubble of the streets, my father came upon Henek and Tulek, and became reunited with Rózia. The four stayed together, shared a room, looked for work. My father found a job at the post office; he was soon promoted to the job of director.

But even this semblance of normality would not last.

"We didn't know if we would ever come out alive. We ran from the Nazis, right into the hands of the Soviets."

Division of Poland at the end of 1939.

Hahray aht m'kudeshet lee b'tahbaht
Zoh k'dat Mosheh v'Yisrael

Behold, you are consecrated to me with this ring
according to the law of Moses and Israel.

Hebrew marriage vow

6

Marriage

For my sixteenth birthday, my parents gave me a birthday party, a "sweet sixteen," as was the custom among my American friends in Chicago. In my circle, to mark the milestone birthday, parents gave their daughters a piece of jewelry, perhaps a ring. My parents wanted me to have everything my friends had, so, from an acquaintance of theirs, they got the name of a jeweler who would give us a good price.

One morning shortly before my birthday, my mother, father and I entered the fifth floor of an office building in Chicago's "Loop." The jeweler placed a tray of rings before me. I tried on several and chose a pinky ring of white gold with a swirl of diamond chips. My father and the jeweler discussed price and settled on fifty dollars. Fair, my father said.

The jeweler turned to my mother: "And what about a ring for you?"

"Oh, I don't wear rings, I don't have jewelry."

"You have a wedding ring?"

The jeweler must have seen that my mother wore no jewelry. He must have noted my mother's modest clothes, my father's calloused hands.

"*Ich hob nicht,*" my mother started. She frequently got her languages confused. "I don't have a wedding ring. The war...we never got...I never had...a wedding ring."

"Oh, you should have a wedding ring," the jeweler said sympathetically, and before she could protest he pulled out another tray filled with wedding and engagement rings.

My mother looked at the tray. My father looked down and nodded. My mother picked up one ring and then another. She held up two to show my father: an engagement ring with a small diamond in an antique setting, and a wedding ring with a circle of diamond chips. Without a word, he took them and helped her try them on.

My father turned to the jeweler. "How much?"

"Thirty-five dollars for the set." Even I knew this was a surprisingly low price.

My father took out his wallet.

After we left, I was too excited about my own ring to ask any questions.

There are no records of my parents' marriage, no photographs of their wedding.

When I was twenty-one and planning my own wedding, my mother and I were in a bridal shop on Devon Avenue near our home in Chicago. The salesclerk brought out several gowns of white silk, holding them up one by one. My mother helped me put a gown over my head, and I stood on a platform in front of a three-way mirror, adjusting the scalloped neckline, the long white sleeves. "This is the one," I said, sighing. I turned to my mother and slid my finger along the Alençon lace, touching the seed pearls down the front. She adjusted the bodice, nodded. "I like it," she agreed.

"What did you wear? At your wedding?" I asked.

"Who remembers?" Her hand waved me away.

"Tell me about your wedding, Mama," I insisted.

"Ach...We didn't have a party," my mother said slowly. "Everyone was sad. We, all of our friends, were worried about our families. When would we see them? What was happening? There was no celebration." Pause. "We just had a rabbi."

❧

My parents always said they were married in Tarnopol. They gave the date as September 1, 1940.

In the Shoah video, the interviewer asks my father: "When were you married?"

"People didn't get married. You didn't know if you would live or die, everyone was dying around you. You lost your family, your friends. If you found someone, you lived together, you didn't think you would survive the next moment."

After I saw the video, in 1996, I phoned him. My mother was dead. He was living in Florida and would die a few weeks later.

"Were you and mother ever married?"

"Of course."

"But on the video you said people just came together?"

"During the war. We didn't know. Would we live or die? We didn't have a wedding. No celebration. Just a rabbi. That's all."

"When? Where?"

"Ukraine. In the war. September 1, 1940."

❧

I thought I understood why my parents were evasive about their marriage. My family did not discuss Ukraine and what happened to them after. In fact, their immigration papers state they were married in Jasło, Poland, on September 1, 1940. I knew they were not there then. I knew why they claimed they were married in Jasło and didn't talk about other places. I thought I had all the answers.

Among my father's papers, after his death, I found a thin tissue paper, a carbon copy of an official-looking document written in German. It was a sworn statement made by my mother and father before the notary Dr. Anton Schmitt, at his office in Fürth, Germany, on November 11, 1947. Dr. Schmitt attests that Herr Moses Rieger and Frau Rosalie Rieger, née Gans, "declared that they wished to give a sworn statement, to give the facts to an official."

It read: "We were married on September 1, 1940, at the marriage bureau in Jasło, Poland. It was the first marriage for both." There was a recitation of the places and dates of each of their births, and, "Currently we cannot provide a marriage certificate."

Tulek and Henek were witnesses: "We can confirm the validity of the previous statements, as the declarers are our sister and brother-in-law."

My mother and father asked for five certified copies of the document for which they paid nineteen reichsmark. The document was signed and sealed.

I knew about this document. In the DP camp in Fürth, when we were recreating our history, the fact of my parents' marriage in Jasło would be evidence that we had not been in the Soviet Union, would prove to the Americans in the midst of the "Red Scare" and witch hunts for Communists that we were not the enemy, and would help us get into the United States.

I knew about the change of place. I never thought to question the date of September 1, 1940, or the fact of a marriage.

September 1, 1940, exactly one year after the Nazi invasion of Poland. They said they didn't remember how long they were in Ukraine, in Lwów, Tarnopol. They didn't remember when they were captured and taken from Tarnopol. But they gave this date. Were they still in Tarnopol on that date?

Now, I was determined. I called Helen.

"Why does it matter?" she answered. "They could have been married anyplace, anytime. In Russia, you paid one ruble and poof, you were married."

Their friend, Yetta Rosenberg, might know. She was there, in the same city, Tarnopol.

I phoned Chicago. Just in time, because she would die within the year. I had to work fast to reach the few elderly survivors who had known my parents during the war.

Yetta recognized my voice. "It's Rieger's daughter," she said in an aside to her husband.

"You were there, weren't you?" I asked. "You were there when my parents were married?"

"No," she replied in a strong voice. "I was there when Tulek got married."

"That was in Chicago. How about my parents? In Ukraine?"

"No," she replied. "I don't know when they were married."

"But you knew them in Ukraine at the time they were married?" I persisted.

"I knew them. They were single." Emphasis on the word single. "We were in Tarnopol. I became friends with your father. I worked for the telephone company. The post office, where your father worked, was in the same building.

"Your mother and father were not married then. They were together. By the time I saw them again in 1945, they were back from Siberia, they had you. I don't know when they got married."

Nad Babim Yarom shelest dihkh trav,
Dyerevya smotryat grozno,
Po-sudeiski.
Zdes molcha vsyo krichit,
I, shapku snyav,
ya chuvstvuyu,
Kak myediemo sedeyu.
I sam ya,
kak sploshnoy bzvuchny krik,
Nad tysyachami tysyach pgrebyonnykh.
Ya—
kazhdiy zdes rasstrelyanni starik.
Ya—
kazndy zdes rasstrelyanny rebyonok.
Nichto vo mne
pro eta ne zabudet!

Wild grasses rustle over Babi Yar.
The trees look stern, as if in judgment.
Here all scream silently, and, removing my hat,
I feel my hair turning gray.

And I myself am one massive, soundless scream
above the thousands of thousands buried here.
I—
am every old man here shot to death.
I—
am every child here shot to death.

Nothing in me will ever forget!

from "Babi Yar" by Yevgeny
Yevtushenko

7

※＊※

The Cattle Cars

IN TARNOPOL, THE SOVIETS required all who were not locals of the area to register and declare whether they would stay or return home. Mundek, Rózia, Tulek, and Henek believed that, when the Nazi threat was over, they would go home.

"We wanted to go home," my father said.

"The Russians told us we would be able to return. So, we registered. We said we were from the west, Poland. We wanted to go back: Henek to his wife and child, we to our homes, to our lives.

"We didn't know"

They didn't know the Soviets would brand them as enemies. After they registered, it was too late. Registration was a trap. The Soviets went after those who had come from the west.

"We heard they were rounding up men. We thought they would not take women."

Mundek, Rózia, Tulek, and Henek shared a sparsely furnished room with a trapdoor to a cellar. The men hid in the cellar and my mother covered the trapdoor with rag rugs. She remained upstairs, alone.

The Soviet soldiers came at night. They surrounded the building and looked for my family, who had registered to go back, the "enemy."

Finding only Rózia, one of the soldiers lifted her off her feet and started carrying her out the door. At the top of her lungs, she shouted "*M'nempt meh!*" Yiddish for "They're taking me!"

Hearing that, Mundek, Henek, and Tulek burst out of the cellar.

"What did we think? That we could save her from the entire Russian army?" my father asks sardonically in the Shoah video.

"They took us all. They got us, every one. They gave us a few minutes to gather some belongings and took us by open truck to the train station.

"They put us into a train of wagons, cattle cars—maybe one hundred people in our wagon. We were kept in the wagons for, how long, no one knows, I think a week. We didn't know what was going on, if we would be killed or what. The Russians provided nothing, no water, no food. The wagons were locked from the outside and the train was heavily guarded. If someone came to the window to give water, the soldiers chopped the person's hands off and killed him on the street.

"We did everything a human being can do in that wagon. We lived and died in that wagon. It was not human."

And then, my father told me:

"From the small window, I saw my brother Sine running toward the wagon. He heard I was being held on the train and he came from the nearby town of Podwołoczysk. He didn't know what was happening; he heard a rumor that we were going back to our hometowns in Poland. The Russians spread this rumor to look for people who were not loyal to the Russians, who were the enemy. Sine was shouting that he wanted to go home. I shouted as loud as I could, warning him. '*Nie! Nie lec.*' 'Don't run. Stay away, we're dying. They'll kill you. We're not going home.' He stopped and didn't get on the train. The Russians didn't pick him up."

My father never saw Sine again. He told me this story only once.

"Sine," he mused. "As children, we called him 'Tasmania' because of his big hair. He liked the outdoors, climbing in the mountains. He studied philosophy."

After a week, the train started to move.

"We didn't know where to."

I think of my scholarly father, my young mother, the dreams they had. I study the history of deportations from the Ukraine. My parents were among thousands of Jews and Poles who were targeted by the NKVD, the Soviet secret police, as enemies of the Soviet regime, because they came from Poland, regardless of the reason. These "enemies" were forcibly transported by the NKVD and Soviet soldiers to prisons or forced labor camps in Siberia, a system that became known as the Gulag. There were four primary waves of deportations of Jews and Poles from Ukraine in 1940 and 1941; most Jews who came from Poland were taken in deportations between February and June of 1940.

Searching for answers, I write to the Polish Committee of the Memorial Society in Moscow:

> I am searching for information about four Polish Jewish persons who were deported from Tarnopol in Ukraine in 1940 to a labor camp in Sverdlovsk. I believe they were deported without any sentence and remained in the labor camp until sometime in 1941.
>
> I would like to know when and where they were taken, how long they were kept, and any other information that is available.
>
> The following is the information I have about the four persons: . . .

Fifteen months pass. A small thick envelope arrives, covered in odd-looking stamps. It contains several certificates in Russian and a letter in Polish. The first certificate, from the Russian Ministry of the Interior from the Region of Sverdlovsk, states: "*Naftali Israelevich Gans, born 1915, sister Rozali Israelevna Gans, born 1914, brother*

Jeheskiel Israelevich Gans, born 1908… sent away on the basis of the decision of NKVD of the region of Tarnopol in 1940, from the town of Tarnopol to the oblast of Sverdlovsk, region of Tugulimsky, the village of Pierwomajski."

A second certificate, also from the Russian Ministry, states: *"Mojzes Israelevich Rieger, born 1912… sent away on the basis of the decision of NKVD of the region of Tarnopol from 1940 from the town of Tarnopol to the Sverdlovsk oblast to the town of Tugulym.*

These two certificates puzzle me. I thought the four were always together. Why was my father's certificate separate? If my parents were married, why was she processed with her brothers and not her husband? Was my father sent to a different place, or is it just the use of language I don't understand? If they were processed separately, when and how did they reunite?

The envelope also contains a letter from the Polish Committee of the Memorial Society in Moscow, summarizing the two certificates I've already read and concluding: *"And so the certificates confirm the fact of the deportation of the family Rieger-Gans… from February 1940…"* But the certificates give no such month of deportation, just the year of 1940.

8

Siberia

"THE RUSSIAN SOLDIERS TOLD us nothing," my father continued. "They came once a day and threw a bucket into the window, water with pieces of dried-up potato swimming in it; they called it potato soup. They told us to throw the dead out the window. There were no other arrangements. There was no toilet, no water, no washing. We couldn't get away. It was no way to live. It was no way to die.

"When the train finally stopped, we knew where we were. The worst place in the world."

Siberia.

※

"The guards came to our wagon and pushed everyone out. We saw only trees, emptiness, nothing, and—cold!"

They were taken to a forced labor camp east of the Ural Mountains in Sverdlovsk Oblast in western Siberia, approximately 3,000 kilometers (1,900 miles) west of Tarnopol.

The four of them, together with others, were herded into a barrack, described by my father as "a barnlike structure with no beds, just a long wooden bench covered with straw where everyone slept.

There were no partitions, everything was open. The only water was in a metal can in the corner. There were no washrooms. Hygiene—forget it.

"Tough guards with rifles and dogs watched over us day and night. We were expected to work from the moment of daylight until dark. At first light, we were sent to the woods to chop trees. But we were given no directions. How to find the place of work and where to go? It was up to us."

The forced laborers, men and women, were formed into battalions of six. The battalions were given a quota of trees per day. My father described the work: "Chop the trees down, chop the branches, saw the logs to pieces, one meter long, and stack the lumber. The more stacks we made, the more bread we got. So they said. But, mostly, we each got one slice of dark bread, dried out, and water with remnants of potato sliding around, what they called soup.

"Many days, we worked in snow and, when it melted, in icy water up to our knees. We never did it before. Some were killing themselves with an axe.... In the winter, especially, your hand slipped on the ice. How many times people chopped off their hands or their feet because they slipped.... There was nobody to help. You just laid down right there and died."

But they were together. Tulek always joked that the four were processed as two couples: Mundek with his wife Rózia was one couple. But the administrators of the *lager* mistakenly took Tulek's formal name, Naftali, as the feminine Naftalia, so Tulek was processed as Henek's wife. This worked to their advantage because women were given a lower quota of wood to chop, and the four together had to chop less wood for their rations.

Henek lost his will. He worried about his wife and child and grieved that he could not return to them. He could not work. Tulek and Mundek chopped the required quotas for all four.

Many around them died, frozen, maimed, hungry, or ill with typhus and dysentery.

My mother became ill. When working in the woods, "She couldn't take it," my father said. "Her legs didn't hold her, she kept falling down." She went to the doctor at the lager who turned her away, but she kept going and, after a while, was released from chopping trees. She was put to work in the kitchen washing floors. "But, still, she was sick all the time," my father said. Now I wonder, could she have been pregnant? Is that why the camp doctor put her in the kitchen? Was this early on and did she miscarry? Or was this later, when she was pregnant with me but told nobody?

My father, on the contrary, became stronger. "I had to be strong. I was a very strong man. I had to stay healthy; I had to stay alive, to keep us all alive.

"The human mind is the richest thing in the world. It can pull you through everything."

❦

My father was always a little proud that he was among the strongest in that environment. He kept a photo of a group of laborers who had exceeded production goals, even though he was later wary of evidence that he'd been in Siberia. In the photo, he is one of a dozen tough-looking men and women, one holding a rifle. Mundek is lean and taller than the others. This photograph must have been taken in summer because there is no snow.

Most of the year it was bitterly cold. "You tried to take a deep breath and couldn't, it hurt," cousin Oskar told me. The three young cousins, Oskar, David and Selma, had been united with their mother after Tulek put them on a train from Jasło to Buczacz. From there, they had fled east, like my parents, and were also forcibly taken by the Soviets. They were in a different labor camp in Siberia. "You'd gasp," Oskar explained. "People smacked their bodies to keep warm, wrapping their arms across their chests and hitting their sides, backs."

The laborers were given special winter clothes, my father said: "Boots that came to the thigh filled with felt. Heavy long pants. *Fufaika*, heavy parkas filled with down and felt. Left open, you would freeze. Hats, felt, all over the head. Only a bit of nose and eyes were

Labor camp in Siberia. My father is at center back, wearing glasses.

left exposed. Otherwise you didn't have a nose. When you spit, it froze. A finger out of your glove, you'd lose it." The temperature went to 50 degrees below zero, and even lower.

In the camp that held my mother, father, and uncles, there was friendship, my father said: "People realized the importance of working together and helping each other. If someone died or was killed, he was one of ours, we lost one of ours, so we had to work together." And then he had a sudden thought: "Come to think of it, they were all Jewish. I don't know how that came to be. I didn't think of it before. Just talking it came out. We were all Jewish in the Siberian lager."

How long were they there? He couldn't remember. "It's always winter except maybe three to four months, June, July, August. Nothing can grow in that climate, even potatoes are difficult. If you want potatoes, the planting must be done before winter ends; the frozen ground must be chopped, then you plant, then you wait a few months for the thaw, for the potatoes to come up, before the next year's freeze."

The camp was miles from anywhere, the terrain and weather forbidding. Anyone trying to run away would have no food, shelter, or water, no identification papers.

"We couldn't leave. By daylight we had to work. There were guards all around. It was important to stay with the family, to stay together."

There was a small farming village many kilometers from the camp. The laborers learned they might get milk or butter there but they had to find something to barter and they had to go at night when they didn't work and might evade the guards. "We took turns going. It was very far and difficult; we didn't know the route or how to go. There were no roads, it was all wildwoods. The thing was to get there and then come back."

They developed a plan so they wouldn't get lost. They stationed people every hundred meters or so and went by relay, one calling to the other, at night in the dark. "It was dangerous and difficult. We lost a lot of people." After evading the guards, those attempting to get to the farm village faced other dangers, animals in the woods. "The wolves were dangerous, foxes, bears, others, whatever you can think of. They didn't spare you."

Few people offered to go more than once. But my father went many times. "They thought I was a good leader. I came back. I was lucky."

My father had a suit. "I carried it with me from Ukraine. Did I think I would go dancing?" He took the suit to the village and traded it for a few pieces of bread. He risked his life for bread, potatoes, milk.

❦

I picture my father, mother, uncles, sliding through deep snow in morning darkness, too numb to feel, then each wielding an end of a heavy saw through frozen tree trunks, standing knee-deep in frost, working through light to darkness, and trudging back exhausted, starved, to slurp lukewarm water with moldy potato, lying down head to toe on a hard plank in a fetid room, then repeating the next morning, each day getting weaker and more hopeless. Why was this done to them? The Holocaust in Europe has been explained as the consequence of a psychotic Hitler and his madmen who demonized Germany and terrorized Europe with their demented belief in the master race and *judenrein*. But why this Soviet brutality? Historians explain that Soviet mass terror was rooted in Russian history under the czars, that Stalin used brutality and forced labor for economic production to build and industrialize Russia, that guards and administrators were corrupt, that law held no limits for the NKVD, that all of the Soviet Union was starving. But why? Why my family, who only wanted a normal life?

9

Buying a Train

MY FATHER AND OTHERS in the lager knew they could not survive the harsh conditions much longer.

"We had to escape. There was no other end."

While my family was focusing on how they might escape from the lager, the war continued to rage in Europe and elsewhere, but alliances of the countries had shifted. On June 22, 1941, Nazi Germany attacked the Soviet Union, putting an immediate end to the nonaggression treaty that had been signed between the two countries in August of 1939. The attack propelled the Soviet Union to the side of the western allies, Britain, France, the already destroyed Poland, and others. The Soviet Union could no longer call Polish persons the enemy, and it needed all the help it could get in the fight against the Nazis. As a result, a month after the Nazis' attack, on July 30, 1941, the Soviet Union signed a treaty with the Polish government in exile and the Soviets declared amnesty for Polish citizens in prisons and labor camps inside the Soviet Union.

The news was slow in reaching most of isolated Siberia, and many in forced labor camps or prisons were not told of the amnesty. For those who were told, there was no implementation; persons in the camps had no way to leave, no papers of authorization or identification, no destination, direction, transportation, funds, or food.

But the situation for Polish Jews like my parents was further complicated. Several months after declaring the amnesty, the Soviet government announced that Jews were not part of this amnesty. My mother and father, Tulek, and Henek, were still not free.

〰

My father spoke about their escape from Siberia. They developed a plan: "We had some very intelligent people in the lager. One was a man named Dr. Künsler, another was an engineer, I forgot his name. They were thinking; they came up with a plan. A few older people had jewelry they had managed to hide. We pooled the jewelry.

"The five who spoke the best Russian stole out of the camp and walked to the nearest town where there was a train station. Those remaining in the lager covered for the five and did their work. The five were smart; they knew what they were doing. With the jewelry they bought a train."

I heard this story of escape from my father and uncles in my earliest years, and I learned more over time. In those days in the Soviet Union, the trainmaster would operate a train from the beginning of its route to the final destination, a journey that could take many months. When my father said they bought a train, it meant they bribed the trainmaster, the engineers, the conductors, and also stationmasters along the way.

〰

It was a freight train loaded with coal. Railroad tracks ran close to the camp, on which rode trains bringing supplies and laborers, as they had brought my family. One night, the bought train stopped on those tracks, as arranged. In the dead of night, two hundred men and women from the camp somehow managed to evade the guards and crept onto the train, burying themselves in the coal-laden freight cars.

"The train moved," my father continued. "We traveled far away. They couldn't find us. The stations didn't have our train's schedule. They didn't know our direction. We just went."

My family and the other escapees wanted to go home, to Poland. But they could not travel west to the border because heavy battles were being fought with the Nazis in those portions of Russia that bordered Europe.

Their second goal was to leave Siberia and get warm. South was warm. But they couldn't go in a straight direction, for fear of being caught and because they had to find goods and survival as they fled. So, they invented as they went along. They caused the train with coal to chug to an area where coal was scarce. There they might sell the coal and buy a commodity plentiful in the new area. "When we got to a station, a few men went ahead on foot to check if it was clear to bring in the train, if we could buy off the *natchalniks*, the stationmasters. If one couldn't be bought, we went back and found another way. We had to buy off everyone. In Russia, at that time, there were great shortages, people had nothing. If you had something, you could buy off anyone."

In the certificates and letter I received from the Russian Ministry of the Interior from the Region of Sverdlovsk and from the Polish Committee of the Memorial Society in Moscow, which told me where my family had been sent, there was additional information. The documents stated that "On August 31, 1941, under the amnesty, as Polish citizens they left to live freely in the Republic of Kyrgyz, the town of Dzhambul." It is possible that this is what happened, and my family was freed and told to go to Dzhambul however they could. In that case, the story of escape would still be true, would be the way they got out of the camp and made their way south.

However, it is also possible that these documents do not specifically address the situation of my family, Polish Jews, from their lager, but are form letters sent to people searching histories of Polish relatives. And I believe the direction of my family, south and eventually to Dzhambul, was, at least in part, coincidental, and somewhat helped by mass migrations and the confused state of travel in Russia at the time. Otherwise, how to explain my family's constant fear of being found and sent back to Siberia, their constant evasion of authorities, their language of escape, their constant hiding?

As an aside, the documents I received state that Dzhambul was in the Republic of Kyrgyz. This was a frequent reference at the time. In fact, the borders between the Soviet Socialist Republics were artificially created in the 1920s and 1930s; Dzhambul was in the Republic of Kazakhstan, close to the Kyrgyz border, and the area may at one point have been part of Kyrgyz.

℘

Those who had escaped the lager zigzagged their way across Russia.

"We traveled east," said my father. "I don't know the dates, I don't know for how long. You name the place, we were there, all the places of the world. We stopped near Novosibirsk. We went south, around Mongolia, China."

They sold the coal. They bought vodka, sugar, salt. They bought in one place where a commodity was plentiful. Then their train stopped where that commodity was in short supply, they sold it and bought a different commodity. "On the black market, everyone tried to sell anything they had to buy food, coal, necessities," my father explained. "We planned everything carefully, we learned how to deal, anything to survive.

"For food, we stopped before a city. We didn't go into the city. We sent a few people, they sold something. Each person went to a different section of the city. We didn't want to sell or buy everything in one place; we didn't want anyone to ask questions, to be suspicious. When our people came back with food, the train started again. We looked for the next place.

"We kept going."

The men became adept at dealing on the black market. "Don't ever sell your coin collection," years later Tulek admonished his ten-year old son, Ira. "A gold coin is the most valuable thing you can have on the black market. Especially good crossing borders."

I heard the same thing from my mother when I was growing up. "Keep jewelry," she'd say, "You can exchange a ring for bread."

As my family shuttled around on trains across the Soviet Union, many other people were also migrating, north to south, west to east, east to west. Poles released from the Gulag to Central Asia were making their way south. Some were struggling to find their way and join a division of the Polish army that was being formed in Uzbekistan.

This direction of many Poles, too, coincided with my family's eventual plan. They were determined to find a way out of the Soviet Union. As they traveled south, however indirectly over thousands of kilometers, they planned to find a way to cross the border where the Central Asian Republics met Persia. Their hope was that from Persia they could get to Palestine, and from there, somehow, become reunited with their families in Poland. The state of Israel had not yet been formed but many Jews lived there.

Persia had been renamed Iran in 1935, but the old name continued. During the war years, when my parents hoped to escape through that country, the British and Russians controlled Persia and it was one of the most important supply routes to Russia.

I now spread out the map of the Soviet Union, a vast region that straddles Europe and Asia. The map itself takes up the entire surface of my desk. The Union of Soviet Socialist Republics, the USSR or Soviet Union, until it broke up on December 31, 1991, was composed of fifteen Soviet Socialist Republics. Russia was the largest and most dominant, stretching from Europe across Asia to the Pacific, and encompassing most of Siberia. Because of its dominance, the names Russia and Soviet Union were frequently used interchangeably, by my family at least.

Five of the Republics were in Central Asia: Uzbekistan, Turkmenistan, Tajikistan, Kyrgyzstan, and Kazakhstan. In 1941, when my father, mother, and uncles, among countless others, were fearfully finding their way or being forced to Central Asia, the borders between the Republics were new and in some ways still being defined. Many natives of the area, such as the Kazakhs, were nomadic, moving across the Central Asian deserts and steppes, from east to west, to Persia and back; under Stalin they were being forcibly settled. Other native groups, such as the Uzbeks, had created imposing ancient cities, Bukhara and Samarkand. Most of the natives of Central Asia were Moslem and of Turkic stock.

On the map, I follow crosshatched lines, representing railroad tracks, on what I imagine to be my family's hopscotch flight from the labor camp. I imagine their train moving, first through the city of Sverdlovsk, a major railroad hub. From there, my eyes catch the tracks of the Trans-Siberian railroad. Did their train move east through Omsk, a city that was becoming the center for many people evacuated from western Russia? Did they then continue further east to Novosibirsk, a city I heard my father mention, the third largest city of Russia and a hub for refugees where many trains originated or ended? After riding thousands of extra miles, buying, selling, and buying again, their train must have turned southwest on the Turkestan-Siberian railroad, tracks I follow through mountain passes toward Kazakhstan.

I study the map of Kazakhstan, an area about the size of western Europe, more than one million miles, much of it steppes, vast treeless, level plains. Rugged mountains ring Kazakhstan's southern and eastern borders. My parents would have approached from the north and east, coming to the city then called Alma-Ata, now Almaty, at the foot of the Altai Mountains. Alma-Ata means "father of apples." The Turkestan-Siberia railroad, completed in 1930, connected Alma-Ata to Siberia and resulted in the city's growth.

"A beautiful all-white city," my father described it, "surrounded by apple orchards." During World War II, the city was the main cultural center of Kazakhstan and a center of Soviet moviemaking.

I stay with my map, tracing train tracks west from Alma-Ata, about 450 kilometers to Dzhambul.

Dzhambul "was a big center; we were able to get food. But we didn't want to stop; we went further. We wanted to get out," my father said.

On the map and in my imagination, I continue to trace the journey my fleeing family may have taken. The freight train, my parents in their boxcar with others, continued into Uzbekistan to the capital city of Tashkent. When the train stopped at the large station, they might have dropped to the platform, teeming with refugees, beggars, itinerant traders. Did Tulek run down a narrow winding alley looking for vendors selling bread? Did my father rush past Uzbeks dressed in *shapan*, long quilted coats, searching for someone he could safely bargain with to sell their freight load of flour? Did my mother sit with Henek, sympathetically listening as he spoke about his lost Irana and Iziu while looking out the window and praying that her husband and brother would get back to the train quickly? I imagine their return, mission safely completed, and the train continuing to the ancient city of Samarkand, home of the poet-warrior Tamerlane. They would not have appreciated the majesty and beauty of this city, called "Rome of the East" by poets and historians, focused as they were on survival and flight. Continuing, they might have passed through the ancient learning center of Bukhara, where they would have searched the many bazaars for willing tradespeople.

My reverie with the map continues. I follow the symbols for train tracks into the Soviet Republic of Turkmenistan, to the city of Mari, an oasis in the Kara Kum desert on the Murgab River delta. In this city, my family might have conducted their trades on the black market on a day with the temperature reaching 110 degrees. Did they trade their flour, or sugar, for cloth?

And then I pause as the train tracks south of Mari split into a fork, one line south and east toward Afghanistan. Did their train go to Afghanistan? "The wild mountain men scared us," my father once said. "We went back." Somewhere across a southern border. I didn't ask.

Their train retreated.

My finger traces the train tracks back into Turkmenistan, to Mari, and the other fork, to the south and west along the Persian border. There the train tracks, at least on my map, end.

"We came close to the Persian border," my father said on the Shoah video. "We had a plan how to get away. They're all Mohammedans, they pray in the morning on mats on the floor. During that time, they don't look up for anything. We moved while they were praying, and this is how we would cross the border.

"We came to a big city. We were in the train and we didn't know where to go. We had nothing to eat and we couldn't buy anything. Then we saw a field, grapes, all over. We were hungry; we ran off the train to the field; we stripped the bushes. We ate too many grapes. We got sick. We lay on the ground. We couldn't move.

"Soldiers seemed to be everywhere. We thought they would kill us. None of us could speak the language. We had nowhere to go. We ran back to the train. We felt we couldn't stay in Persia. We had to go back."

They almost made it.

But their train retreated, as do my fingers on the map, back through Turkmenistan, past Mari, to Uzbekistan, back across the southern Central Asian desert, back toward Kazakhstan.

Their train was stopped by a desert sandstorm. My father described: "We saw how people lived. Their homes were round huts. When the storm came, it created a division, like a road. One side was covered with sand, you couldn't see anything. The people on this side just picked up their huts and moved to the other side, setting up their homes again, away from the sandstorm."

My father meant yurts. They're tents that can be easily moved. When they're set up, people put kilims on the walls and on the floor, very cozy inside.

Stopped by the sandstorm, the escapees could go no further. They were back in Dzhambul.

Jazdigun shilde bolganda,
Koukorai shalgyn, baisheshek,
Uzarin ousin tolganda;
Kurkirep jatkan ouzenge,
Koship auil konganda,
Shurkirap jatkan jilkinin,
Shalginnin joni kiltildan,
At, aigirlar, bieler
Buiri shigip, inkildap,
Suda turip shibindap,
Kuirigimen shilpildap,
Arasinda kulin-tai
Ainala shauip bultildap.
Jogari- tomen yuirek, kaz
Uship tyrsa simpildap.
Kiz-kelinshek yui tiger,
Byrala basip bilkildap,
Ak bilegin sibanip,
Azildesip cinkildap.

When summer in the mountains gains its peak,
When gaily blooming flowers begin to fade,
When nomads from the sunshine refuge seek
Beside a rapid river, in a glade,
Then in the grassy meadows here and there
The salutatory neighing can be heard
Of varicolored stallion and mare.
Quiet, shoulder-deep in water stands the herd;
The grown-up horses wave their silky tails,
Lazily shooing off some irksome pest,
While frisky colts go frolicking about
Upsetting elder horses, at their rest.
The geese fly honking through the cloudless skies.
The ducks skim noiselessly across the river,
The girls set up the felt tents, slim and spry,
As coy and full of merriment as ever.

From "Summer" by Abai
Kunanbaev (1845–1904),
Kazakh poet

10

Dzhambul

"Dzhambul is an old city, a very beautiful city," my father said. "The homes are made from earth, how do you call it, *glina?*" Clay—the houses were made of unfired clay bricks. "They have thick walls made of earth, round ceilings, and floors also of earth.

"Dzhambul was a different city from what we knew. They didn't know we were Jewish, I don't think they knew Jews at all. Most of them were Moslem.

"There were very good people in Dzhambul.

"It was not a fantasy land, but it saved us."

Meine ziboleh," my mother would croon when I was a little girl, stroking my head. "You were a blue baby, born feet first with the cord wrapped around your neck. A miracle.

"You were our sign from God that we would be saved."

My mother was pregnant but she told no one. She was so thin and her belly hardly grew, so no one noticed, not even my father, until well into their flight from Siberia, somewhere on that train crisscrossing its way to Central Asia, when she was in her seventh month.

After their odyssey to Persia, the train retreated and stopped in Dzhambul. Shortly after, my mother went into labor.

Almost like a mantra in my childhood, my uncles Tulek and Henek always said my birth saved them. There was a law in Dzhambul, they told me, that any baby born in the city had to be given a place to live. Even my father, never one to exaggerate, chimed in: "We were on the streets. People were dying there, dropping of typhus, dysentery. But you were born and we were given a home."

The house we were to live in was owned by the *hajaika,* as we called her, the Russian word for landlady or homemaker. The hajaika's husband worked on the railroad and was away with his train for months at a time. They had three sons who had been sent as soldiers to the front. So the house had extra rooms and we were told to move in.

We were lucky. We had a place to live.

Me in Dzhambul.

Then we found my mother's young cousins, Oskar, David, and Selma, the three Tulek had put on a train in Jasło when war broke out. They had been reunited with their mother and grandmother in Poland, but all were taken to Siberia in a transport similar to the one that took my family. The children's mother died in the labor camp and their grandmother died in transport. David and Selma, teenagers by then, had landed in the Zhelezno-Dorozhnoy Oochilishche, the Railroad Learning Institute, in Dzhambul. Oskar was in an orphanage in a kolkhoz in Moin Kum, Kazakhstan.

David and Selma were able to leave the Institute for only short periods of time. David usually went to the black market near the railroad station. One day, Selma went to the market. She met some Jewish people. One woman asked her surname.

"Gans," Selma replied.

"There are people named Gans from Jasło living in town," the woman told her.

Selma told David.

"I found the house where you lived with the hajaika," David told me, shaking his head as if still in disbelief. "I remember going there. A mean black dog was in the yard, Zuk." Another shake of his head; no guard dog could deter David. How surprised my parents and uncles must have been to find him on their doorstep! They never described the reunion, but my mother always felt grateful that she had a role in bringing back her small cousins and spoke of Oskar with the affection of a mother. Tulek always boasted that he found the cousins and brought Oskar out of the orphanage.

David gave me a different version. He said that after he found my family he told them that Oskar was still at the orphanage in Moin Kum and asked my parents if they would take him. They agreed—but would the orphanage release him? David, wily and resourceful at fourteen, managed to return by train to Moin Kum, expecting to steal Oskar out of the orphanage. "But the authorities quickly agreed to let Oskar go," David said. "There was no food. The orphans were dying of starvation."

"Dave got me out of the orphanage," Oskar told me. "We stayed in the vestibule of a cargo train half the night. I was so cold, Dave lay on top of me to keep me warm. In Dzhambul, Dave went and got Tulek. They carried me."

When Oskar came to live with us, he was ill with malaria and typhus, and so emaciated that his stomach was swollen. He was twelve. I was two.

Oskar was to stay with us for the next three years. I loved him and followed him around our few rooms. I called him my *braciszek*, little brother. David and Selma visited every day, walking from the Railroad Learning Institute, to eat with us. The Institute "was supposed to be a school," David said, "but we were put to work making parts for machine guns. Anyway, who could learn anything? We were constantly thinking of food."

❧

Getting food was everyone's focus. We didn't have much. The men searched for work, complicated because they had no papers and avoided authorities. Tulek worked the black market. For a time, my father and Henek worked in a flour mill. Many days, they would roll up the cuffs of their trousers and, as they worked, surreptitiously slip flour inside their cuffs. A favorite story, told by my mother and one of the few things she later remembered, was about how, when the men came home, I would run and get a bowl, squat down by my father, put the bowl under one leg, unroll the cuff, and call "*Sip, sip, Tatusiu!*" Pour, pour, Daddy. My father jiggled his leg so the flour came into the bowl. I repeated the routine with his other leg, and then ran with the bowl to Henek.

Oskar remembers grinding the flour: "The hajaika had a stone mill, two stones with a handle. Many nights, I'd be sitting on the floor and grinding."

My mother fooled us into thinking we were eating soup, *zacharka*. "We called it kasha," Oskar said, "but it wasn't buckwheat, it was made with the flour from the mill. After separating out the bugs and dirt, Rózia would put water to boil in a pot and add the flour. It had a consistency like glue. Sometimes, she was lucky and got an onion at the bazaar. Other times, she baked flatbreads, *lepyoshka*, which we ate and shared with the hajaika, or traded for sugar on the black market."

We shared what we could, flour soup or flatbread, with the hajaika. She, in turn, shared with us. In the summer, we could pick apples or apricots from a tree in her small orchard. She gave us milk from her cow. We made yogurt, *kwasne mleko*, from the milk. When I became old enough to toddle around, I'd take my tin cup to the hajaika as she milked the cow, and she'd aim the teat right into the little cup, filling it with warm, foaming milk.

We learned to churn butter. The hajaika had a manual centrifuge. She poured milk into the bucket and it filtered down. As you stirred, the milk separated from the cream; then it got lumpy and you fished out the butter. The remaining liquid was thin, like nonfat milk.

"We were very lucky the hajaika had that cow," my father said. He used the milk to make ice cream to sell on the black market. "People loved it."

"How did you know how to make ice cream?" I asked.

"When you have to, you learn."

Recently, I met an elderly man in Chicago, a Polish Jew who was in Dzhambul during the war years, a refugee like my family. I asked him how he survived.

"I found whatever work I could," he told me.

"For example?"

"In 1944, I worked in an ice-making plant. We made ice which was used in train cars. There was no refrigeration, ice was the only way to keep meat and other things cold. We made it in the winter, put a large mound of snow into the cellar and kept pouring water over it; the water would freeze and we had a growing chunk of ice. We covered it to keep it cold. I made an arrangement with the owner of the plant and the guards; I paid them off so I could get some of the ice. I broke off smaller chunks, put them in bags, and sold the ice on the black market. I had to do this at five in the morning, and the buyers had to use the ice quickly before it melted."

"Who did you sell the ice to?" I asked, holding my breath.

"I sold some to a Jewish man who used it to make ice cream."

"That was my father!" I shouted. "Do you remember his name? Rieger?"

"No, sorry, I don't remember.

"I sold the ice to a man on the bridge over the train tracks. He would walk in one direction, I in the other, we'd meet and the ice and money would change hands quickly.

"It was dangerous," the man continued. "We had to be very careful. Under Communist law, speculation, making a profit was forbidden. A *spekulant* would be arrested and given seven years. We used to joke, if arrested, tell them: 'I didn't buy, I didn't sell, I stole it.' You only got one year for stealing."

Now I imagine my father, waking at four a.m., walking a few kilometers to the bridge, his last few kopeks in his pocket, keeping an eye out for police as he bought ice and returned quickly home to make ice cream.

"He included some powdered egg product and cooled the mixture overnight in the hajaika's cellar," Oskar explained.

"Where did the powdered egg come from?" I asked.

"It came from the good old US of A as part of all the assistance to the war effort that Uncle Sam was sending to the Red Army. Some of these goods always seemed to trickle down to the starving citizens via the black market.

"Sometimes I helped your father sell near the train station. Your father filled a square-shaped plunger-type scoop with the ice cream and pushed it out onto a square piece of paper, then covered it with a same-size paper to form an ice cream sandwich."

We lived about three kilometers from the train station, down a sandy road wide enough for two horse-drawn carts to pass each other. Oskar described it to me.

The house and its grounds were surrounded by a post and wire fence. We entered through two gates: first, a slatted gate led to the apple orchard, about three acres in size. Twenty yards in, a second, heavier gate opened onto the house and adjacent yard. The yard held a barn just large enough for the cow at one end, an open shed at the other, and an outhouse in the middle.

The hajaika had a big black dog named Zuk, a spitz, which is a hunting dog often used as a guard dog because it doesn't take to strangers. Zuk was on a chain that reached both gates, to scare away intruders. Mostly Zuk scared my mother and me.

"When we went to the outhouse," Oskar said, "Zuk would bark and follow. We'd make a wide circle; the chain wasn't quite long enough to reach the outhouse, but Zuk would sit there waiting."

The house itself was a one-story adobe with wooden floors. The hajaika kept two rooms for her own use. The main room served as our living room and bedroom; my parents slept on one sofa, Henek on another, and my crib was in the middle. Tulek and Oskar slept on mattresses on a type of enclosed porch. We also had a small side room with an old wood-burning stove for heat and cooking.

From the yard or orchard, we could stand at the fence and talk to people walking by on the street. The hajaika often met with her neighbors this way.

People were always trying to break into the orchard to get apples. The dog would bark and scare them away, and wake us. The hajaika wanted to catch the people trying to break in. She made Oskar go up to the roof of the barn with her to spend the night and look out. They did this three or four times but never caught anyone.

"The hajaika's name was Nyura Peredereeva," Oskar told me when I was preparing to go to Kazakhstan in 2007 to look for traces of my family history. "She was about fifty years old, Russian, not a native Kazakh, short and squat, always in a drab shapeless dress, a babushka covering her brown hair. She worried constantly about her sons in the army and showed us their photos. Whenever she got mail, she crossed herself before opening it. She read us all the letters from her sons. In late 1944, the letters stopped."

After that, the hajaika kept the door to her rooms closed. She began to have visitors, usually three at a time. "One day, she called me into her room," Oskar said. "Turned out she was a fortune-teller. One of her friends didn't show up and she needed my help, a fourth person for the Ouija board. The four of us put our hands on the board, the hajaika would ask a question, 'Will my sons come back from war?' and the pointer on the board moved."

Oskar, Selma, and me. My hair was shaved to get rid of lice.

11

❦

Our Life in Dzhambul

TULEK CAME HOME AFTER a day at the black market carrying his treasures, whooping with delight, boasting about his skill at outwitting the sellers. One day he returned, breathing hard but beaming with pride at the grand prize he carried on his back: a cradle for me. When he retold this story, years later, I always felt it showed his great love for me.

The cradle stood on its rockers in the center of our room from where I commanded everyone's attention. "*Huśtai tak dobrze!*," Rock me, really hard! I'd shout, and one or the other would jump up to rock the cradle, to my delight and laughter, any time of day or night.

Years later, Tulek often told stories about me, to anyone and everyone: my exploits, my cute sayings, and some stories that, as a teenager, made me blush. "She stood on my mattress, this one," he'd say. "She wanted to look out the window. And then—*pish.*" Tulek laughed. "You weren't yet toilet trained. Ach, my mattress." And Tulek laughed and laughed.

My uncles made me the center of attention. For as long as I can remember, whenever anyone came to visit, they showed me off, talked about how clever I was, asked me questions, and puffed with pride at my answers. It felt natural to me, and I always felt I was the luckiest girl in the world.

My uncles loved telling about a little girl who came to play with me. Her mother reported that when the little girl got home, she cried and cried. Her mother was perplexed. "What's wrong?" the mother asked. "What happened at Anusia's house?"

After many tears, the little girl plaintively asked: "Why does Anusia have three daddies but I have only one?"

After that, my uncles called me the girl with three daddies.

I knew I was special.

Henek teased and provoked me with his salty humor. My mother didn't want me to pick up his vocabulary, but he was irrepressible and I learned all his words. A favorite was *dupa*. "Mama, Mama," I'd call, running to my mother. "Henek is using such a big fat dirty word." I spread my arms as wide as I could.

My mother sighed. "Ach, Henek." Henek winked at me conspiratorially.

I mimicked the adults around me and learned to speak articulately by the time I was two. I especially followed Oskar everywhere, sat with him when he studied and memorized the poems he had to learn for school. "You learned them faster than I did," Oskar recently told me. I didn't mention that this was one of my uncles' boasts about me.

"You played with a boy named Salak, from a Polish-Jewish family who lived in the house on the corner next to our house, do you remember?" Oskar asked, but I shook my head. I have no memory of our time in Dzhambul. Tulek said I had playmates from every ethnic group in the neighborhood: Russian, Kazakh, Uzbek, Tajik, and Kyrgyz, and by the time I was three, I spoke each of those languages with my playmates. I don't remember those languages, but I remember knowing that there were different "sets of words" appropriate in different circumstances and some sets of words were not to be spoken at all in some situations.

An itinerant photographer went from house to house. My mother commissioned him to take a picture of me on my first birthday. We barely had food, but photos were important. They had no photos of those left behind. In one sepia-toned photo, I'm sitting on a chair, a blonde toddler with a solemn expression, in an open nightshirt with bare feet. In a second photo, I'm about two, standing on a chair, one hand resting on its back. I'm wearing a light dress, an army logo visible on its sleeve, brown lace-up shoes and dark socks slouched down at the ankles. My blonde hair has grown unruly, and I'm looking out at the world with large solemn eyes.

In the third photograph, taken in the yard of the hajaika's house, I'm standing between Oskar and Selma, who are kneeling so my arms can rest on their shoulders. We're squinting at the sun. My head looks too big for my thin body; my dress is a patchwork of panels. This time, my hair has been shaved. "Lice," my mother said.

My mother used to root through my hair with a special comb looking for lice. *Bibeleh, bibeleh lazeleh,"* she singsonged in Yiddish. *"Oifen shteit a hazeleh, hinten shteit a bonk, knik, knak, knok,"* showing me, on the last *knok,* how she used to smash the lice on the flat edge of the comb with her thumb.

"The lice were fierce. We picked them out of each other's hair, clothes. Most of the time they stayed hidden in the seams of our clothes. When they crawled out and on your clothes it was embarrassing," Oskar said. But, worse than the itch or embarrassment was that lice carried typhus, a disease that causes fever and pain, and occasionally death. We had no medication for it. Typhus was rampant throughout the Soviet Union during that time.

❦

Every man had to work. Men were not permitted to be at home or in town during the day. The police patrolled the streets and houses looking for able-bodied men to conscript for labor or send to the front.

My father and uncles constantly evaded anyone in uniform, for fear that they would be sent back to Siberia or, even if not recognized as escaped Jews, caught and sent for hard labor, *trudavya.* Frequently, the police were given a quota, say fifty young men, and they'd round up whoever they could, take them to the train station, and send them away. These men were shipped to labor camps or road gangs, to railroads, steel mills, coal mines, and factories where war materials were being produced, and frequently never heard from again.

My father constantly carried the fear of being sent away. He developed a deep antipathy to Communists. He had been so affected by his experience in Siberia that he could not trust Soviet authorities, even those in Dzhambul where my family found a sort of respite.

"When they found out I'm college educated, right away they wanted to make me a judge," he said. "I wasn't their enemy, they treated me like I was their best friend, because that's what they wanted to do with me. But I didn't want to join them. After all that had happened, after Siberia, I didn't want to be a Communist. I felt disgusted. I felt degraded. I felt low, after everything that had been done to me.

"I ran away. But they came after me. The Communists didn't give up. They put the army after me. When they came to the house, the hajaika put me on the bottom of the cowshed. They wanted to catch me. They wanted to kill me. First they wanted to give me everything, then they wanted to kill me because I wouldn't accept. And that's life? This is the world? One people enemy to the other one? And this is the way to live?"

There were other incidents I heard about. In one piece of family lore, I was the hero at three years old and saved my father. Once again, the military came looking for him. It was on a day when my father and I were home alone. From the window, my father saw a soldier walking down the road. He told me to say he was not there and quickly went out the side door that led to the cowshed.

The soldier came to the window where I was standing on Tulek's mattress looking out.

"Are you alone, little girl?" the soldier asked.

"Yes," I replied, dutifully. "My mother is at the bazaar and my father is at work."

"Are you afraid to be alone?"

"No."

"Are you really all alone?"

"Yes and I don't like being alone. Won't you stay with me?"

"Hmm...Well, tell your parents not to leave you alone again."
The soldier left.

After that, and for the rest of our stay in Dzhambul, my father continued to evade authority. The military, police, soldiers, they were all one and the same in our minds.

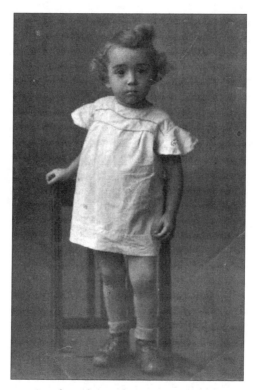

Another photo of me in Dzhambul.

Capitalism, private enterprise, was forbidden, and consumer goods were scarce, but there was an underground black market. In Dzhambul, much of the buying and selling took place around the train station. Tulek spent most of his days working the black market, then regaling us with his success.

"I had an experience," he'd say. "I met another Polish Jew. He directed me to a group. Look what I got." He produced a pair of small brown shoes. As my mother grabbed them to put them on my feet, Tulek turned in my direction. "Grrr..." he growled. He grabbed my arm and took a giant pretend bite. I giggled.

Tulek continued: "The man introduced me to his sister. She was quite nice." At this, Tulek rolled his eyes and my mother flashed a look at me. "We spent the day together. She wants to come with me; she cried when I left. I promised her I'd come back."

"Oh, yes." My mother nodded. "And what about the school-teacher? I thought you were in love with her?"

"Uh." Tulek shrugged. He picked me up and whirled me around.

༄

After that first job at the flour mill, Henek got a job in his old line of work as a printer, at a newspaper in town. "I can work in any language," Henek, never boastful, told me in later years. "I just copy what they give me."

Henek's hands were stained black from the Linotype. He often brought home a copy of the newspaper, *The Dzhambul Communist*. Oskar remembers that it had the Bolshevik slogan in a banner above its name: "*Prolytariy ysekh straan, soyedinyaityes!* Workers of all the lands, unite!"

Oskar went to a school established by Polish Jews and named after Adam Mickiewicz, a famous nineteenth-century Polish poet whose romantic poems are full of Polish nationalism and yearning for self-determination. "I never learned Kazakh history," Oskar told me. "We learned about Russia and Poland, but not Kazakhstan."

༄

Before 1920, the population of Kazakhstan was sparse and largely nomadic. Most were Moslem. In the 1930s, the Soviet government wanted to develop the area agriculturally and moved large groups of people into kolkhoz, collective settlements. At the same time, the Soviets established prisons and forced labor camps in Kazakhstan, as they did in Siberia, and sent political enemies to this remote region. When the prisoners were released, many remained. During the second world war, the Soviets sent Poles, Ukrainians, and others into exile in this remote region, and people like my family found themselves here under varying circumstances. By the early 1940s, the exiles became a majority and the native Moslem population declined to less than 50 percent.

Religion was suppressed under the Soviet regime. When we were in Dzhambul, there were no mosques or muezzins calling the Moslems for prayers. We remained quiet about our own religion. We rarely spoke Yiddish. We didn't celebrate Sabbath or holidays. The hajaika never knew we were Jewish. Neither her friends, the Russians who were her neighbors, nor the Kazakhs knew. "We worried about Russians and Ukrainians," Oskar said, "but never about the local Moslems." Other Jews knew we were Jewish, though, and my family had frequent interaction with them at bazaars and other places.

~

Dzhambul was in an arid desert region of Kazakhstan, with extreme temperatures, very hot in the summer, bitter in winter. Because it was dry, irrigation ditches were common. One *arochok* cut a deep channel of water a few blocks from the hajaika's house. My mother would do our laundry in the arochok, carrying the bundle down the sandy road, immersing each shirt or sheet, beating it with a stone, wringing out the water. Then she'd carry the laundry home and hang it on a rope strung up between two poles in the yard.

She always took me to the arochok and washed our clothes while I played nearby. One day, as she worked, a large snake suddenly appeared at her feet. She screamed and jumped, and her heart pounded until the snake slithered away.

Another time, my mother couldn't find me at home. At first, she thought I was picking apples with the hajaika, but when I didn't appear, she looked for me in the street. She became panicky. She called for me. She ran up and down the street, to the arochok, shouting. She ran back to the house, crying for help. The hajaika and others came out and searched for me. Hours passed. My father and uncles came home from work and joined in the search. At dusk, the neighborhood men brought out heavy equipment and began dredging the arochok for my body.

My father and uncles refused to give up. They continued to search, door-to-door, into outlying streets, trying every house. Finally, they found me at the home of a Kazakh playmate where I had wandered.

꧁

Living in close quarters permitted little privacy.

Henek was depressed over the loss of his wife and son. "The last time I saw Iziu he was five years old," Henek would tell any visitor. "My wife and I became separated..." He choked. "On Passover, my wife set a beautiful table, with our best dishes and glasses. Remember Rózia?"

My mother nodded, starting a small smile, knowing what was coming.

"One time, I took Iziu to a magic show in Kraków," Henek continued. "When my wife set the Passover table a few days later, with all our best dishes and glasses on a white tablecloth, Iziu wondered if he could do the magic trick just like the magician, pull out the tablecloth while all the dishes stayed in place. Before anyone could stop him, Iziu yanked the starched white cloth. Everything..." And Henek laughed. He laughed and laughed. He couldn't stop. He put his hands over his face. His whole body shook. Everyone became very quiet, even me.

꧁

When Henek wasn't mourning, he joked and teased, or came

home with another sardonic expression. *"Pies psu ucha nie ugrizie,"* he might say. "One dog wouldn't bite another's ear."

Tulek, too, was a jokester, but one who created action and disturbances around him. He was always ready to fight. My mother would try to bring him in line. As a result, our household was filled with intense arguments and lots of yelling.

Tulek was always shouting. "Tulek was very difficult," my mother told me shortly before she died. She never spoke ill of her brothers, but "he made me sick in Dzhambul," she said. "That's what made me sick." But she didn't elaborate.

"I know you loved him," Oskar told me more recently, "but Tulek made me sick in Dzhambul. I was afraid to complain." He, too, didn't elaborate.

My father, unlike my uncles, was introspective. "Your dad always took great care of your mom. He was protective," Oskar told me. "I wanted to be like him. He was educated, the smart one, intellectual. With the family he was reserved, staying out of the way and out of the fights. His quiet sense of humor was overwhelmed when the others were around. Sometimes, a smile cracked his face when he was sitting with them, as if he thought of something humorous.

"I think Mundek felt trapped," Oskar concluded. "He was always talking about Persia, how to get out."

℞

In 1942, a division of the Polish army was permitted by the Soviets to organize in Uzbekistan, then cross the border into Persia to join the fight against Nazi Germany.

"We went to the Polish army and volunteered," my father said. "I told them who I was, that I had a right to be there because I'm Polish, I'm educated in Polish schools. But, no, they wouldn't take us Jewish people."

In fact, I now learn that some Jews were able to join and fight with the Polish troops against the Nazis. But others, like my family, were stopped either by Soviet authorities or by Poles. I have read that the Poles were afraid that if other minorities joined, the Polish army would not be permitted to leave the Soviet Union. In any event, in March of 1943, the potential for anyone to escape from the Soviet Union by joining the Polish army was closed. The Soviet government revoked its amnesty for Poles in the Soviet Union and Poles were no longer permitted to form their own army.

❧

Selma, David, and Oskar also dreamed of getting out. They wanted to go to America; their father was there; he would take care of them. "He'll want us, he'll love us, he's waiting for us," they'd say over and over. And no one contradicted them.

❧

My mother, too, longed to get out of the Soviet Union and go home. My mother was able to write to her mother from Siberia and later from Dzhambul and received a few replies as late as 1944. The letters were sent through Teheran. My mother knew that her mother, Debora, was being hidden by neighbors in their hometown of Jasło. "She knew you were born," my mother told me. "I thought she was still alive."

❧

In Dzhambul we got little news of the war. The newspaper Henek brought home told of Soviet victories but gave little account of events in Europe.

On February 2, 1943, the fierce, bloody, and long protracted, battle of Stalingrad ended with a Nazi surrender to the Soviets. After that, the war shifted. After that, the Nazi army was in retreat.

"There were no government pronouncements that the war was coming to an end," my father said. "We could tell that the war was ending only by the number of soldiers coming back from the front."

"But when the war did finally end, we knew it," Oskar told me in later years. "There was a big celebration in the stadium in Dzhambul several days after VE day—Victory in Europe, May 8, 1945. I went, everybody went, except you and your mom. David was there with the Railroad Institute band, he played trombone. There was so much excitement, martial music, dancing among the spectators, total rejoicing."

'Then we knew we had to leave," my father said. "We had to leave. We were losing ourselves. It was just a matter of time before the hardships would catch up to us and we would die. I couldn't just stay there.

"We brought together the members of the group who had escaped Siberia, those who were still alive, and asked if they wanted to leave Dzhambul. We got about fifty people. Not everybody wanted to leave; it was too dangerous, they didn't want to go. Some were sick. It was too much for others.

"We made plans to do the same thing as before, like when we left Siberia. We found a train and bought it, bribed the trainmaster, the stationmaster. So, we started the long journey back to Europe, to Ukraine, and to Poland. Home. We hoped."

As best I can determine, my family left Dzhambul in June, 1945.

12

Escape

WE LEFT IN THE middle of the day.
When Oskar and David told me this part of my family's
history, I could not imagine myself in the situations they describe.
I'm an American, interested in clothes and makeup, concerned with
my diet and with the "burden" of too much abundance.

My mother remembered, though. Even after many years in the
United States, my mother would go into a restaurant and laugh out
loud at the sight of packets of sugar on the table. "In Russia, they'd
be gone in an instant."

We left Dzhambul in the middle of the day, eight of us: my father,
mother, Tulek, Henek, our teenaged cousins Oskar, David and Selma,
and me. We left quietly. I don't remember if they explained to me
what was happening, but I knew. Even at the age of three, I understood what they felt and what had to be done.

My father and uncles had made "arrangements" for our journey
on the "501" train. It would go only once a week, Monday or Tuesday.
We didn't know what week, what day, or what time the train we
bought would come. We waited. We discussed a system to notify
each other. As it turned out, our contact found Tulek first and told
him the train was on its way. Tulek went to the Railroad Institute to

fetch David and Selma. David ran into town to the newspaper to get Henek, then to the train station where my father was selling ice cream.

The men arrived home and spoke to my mother, who began packing food. We left quietly, one by one, so as not to alert anyone. We took no luggage, just the clothes on our backs: me in a dress handmade from a man's shirt, my mother in a worn cotton house-dress. We didn't say good-bye to the hajaika. Later, my mother often wondered about her. What did she think when we just disappeared? Did her sons ever come back from the war?

But, at the time, my parents thought only of how to leave. At the *vagsal*, the railroad station, we met the others who would escape with us. The well-used freight train, dusty with desert sand and the dry earth of the steppes, waited at a siding, its engines shut down. We climbed into a boxcar with a few couples, a man with a beard, one woman in makeup. This surprised sixteen-year-old David, trained at the Railroad Institute by Communists. Forbidden, he thought. "She must be a whore."

Our car had no benches or partitions, only a tarpaulin tacked to the roof in the middle, above and surrounding a hole that had been chopped in the floor for a toilet. One boxcar held the commodities we'd bought, sugar beets and wheat flour, which the men would barter as we traveled. My father explained: "Same as when we left Siberia. We bought our way with sugar, salt, with coal we got from Kazakhstan. Salt, which we got in the Caspian lowlands, was better than sugar, than vodka, than anything. Russia didn't have it. You could buy the biggest stationmaster with salt. We paid everyone off."

That summer of 1945 travel was chaos: returning soldiers, reset-tlements, people being sent to Gulags, continued deprivation. Most people didn't know where they were going or how they would get there. But the war in Europe had ended and the authorities weren't watching as closely as before, so we were able to move about. Still, we had no papers permitting us to travel. We were outside the system. Our lives depended on people we could bribe to keep our secret, trainmasters, stationmasters, local officials; on the goodwill of people with whom the men bartered; and even on the girls with whom Tulek flirted.

It took us six weeks to journey from Dzhambul, across Kazakhstan and across Russia. We couldn't go in a direct route. We had to avoid stations where we might be stopped, and had to go out of our way to barter and find food. In addition, two or three times a day, our train had to pull off to a siding and wait as another train passed. In many places, there was only one track on which trains traveled in both directions. If two trains were approaching from opposite directions, the less important train had to pull off. Whenever we stopped, Oskar and I kept watch out the soot-covered window. After the other train passed, we'd wait for our train to start. It took another long fifteen or twenty minutes before we heard the whistle and tug of wheels as the train started and turned back to the main track.

Many of the trains that passed us carried Soviet troops and equipment from Europe to the front with Japan. Sometimes, as we waited at a siding for a train going east to pass, soldiers waved to us from the passing train, and Oskar and I would wave back. "*Och*, don't let them see you," my mother would fret.

Other times, less frequently, a train would pull off for us to pass. These trains usually carried Soviets liberated from German prison camps, labor camps, and factories. Stalin exiled these people to the Gulag, treating them as enemies for permitting themselves to be caught.

Once again, I spread out the map of this vast region. From Dzhambul, I follow one rail line southwest, two hundred kilometers, skirting the mountains along the border with Kyrgyzstan to the city of Chimkent, near the border with Uzbekistan. My family stopped there, perhaps after two days of slow travel.

Chimkent. Many local people flocked to this train station, waiting for hours for any train that might stop, selling whatever they had: a few eggs, bread, milk, in the same way my father had sold ice cream at the train station in Dzhambul. The men had to barter and find food quickly.

In Chimkent, there was a hot water faucet. Hot water, *kipyatok*, was a luxury you could get in only a few stations, in a big city. People took their teakettles and stood in long lines to fill them. Cousin Selma was so excited to get to the hot water, she tripped over a rusty pipe and fell. She has the scar to this day.

From Chimkent, the train tracks on the map turn northwest and start a long trek across the deserts and steppes of Kazakhstan. I imagine our train chugging along at five to ten miles per hour through the Moin Kum Desert, sand broken up here and there by white and black saxaul trees. In some stretches, the train would move through the greener valley of the Syr Darya River. And so we slowly passed five hundred kilometers to the next large city, Kyzylorda, in a fertile rice-growing area. Maybe we bartered there for rice? But how did we cook the rice? How did we eat? We had no plates, no utensils.

"Tulek bartered for a small portable kerosene stove," Oskar explained. It had a pump to create air pressure; the kerosene came up so you could light the wick. We used it to cook potatoes, hard-cooked eggs. Mostly, we ate bread that we got at the stations.

A remembered taste of Russian black bread, dense and stale and it left me with a stomach ache. "You would always find something in the bread: string, small stones and other foreign objects," Oskar said. "The bread was sticky and you could form a slice into a ball when you squeezed it. But it was bread and we ate it."

In this way, I imagine our train continuing slowly northwest, around the Aral Sea, crossing the vast Kazakh steppes, treeless areas of dustbowl and draught. Through the open window of our boxcar, the dry, beige sand and dusky sky framed mile after mile of parched earth where only feather grass grew. In some stretches, we might see a distant herd of wild horses, or flocks of sheep, *Karakul*, watched over by shepherds on horseback; occasionally maybe we saw felt yurts, homes of the nomads of the steppes, and their camels.

We slept side by side on the dirty floor of the boxcar, with whatever we had, coats or sweaters, as mats and cover. When the train stopped, we'd rush to breathe the fresh air, jump off, stretch our legs and find a bush for a toilet—more private than the hole in the floor of our boxcar—and we learned not to startle at the scamper of a marmot or jerboa through the sagebrush.

When the men were lucky they made connections at the train station, heard where they could sell our commodities, then left us to find the potential buyer and negotiate the sale. Oskar told me that those of us left behind waited and worried. Would they come back? Would they be arrested? Would the authorities come and find us on the train? Would the NKVD send us back to Siberia? "We felt relieved when they returned and the engine of our train rumbled and started once again."

Our group of Polish Jews was a community of its own, working together to find the black market, going in different directions. If one family had luck finding a source, they shared with the others. Our family had three men, my father and two uncles—four men, if you counted David—adept at working the black market, so we were often luckier than most.

My mother stayed with me every moment, hovering over me even inside the confines of the boxcar. Not having toys for me to play with, she taught me poems she learned as a child: "*Hupu tsupu, klastu, klastu, nie mam rączek jedenastu,*" "I don't have eleven hands, I only have two small ones, with them I can sew, wash, iron…" And then she added her own revised ending for my benefit: "and do my homework."

Sometimes we played word games to see how many ways we could say the same thing. I was a "little girl," *mała dziewczynka* in Polish, *kleine maidle* in Yiddish, *yaldah* in Hebrew, *devochka* in Russian, and I don't remember Kazakh. My father could be *Tatuś, Ojciec, Abba, Tateh, Papa.* But my mother was always *Mama.*

On the train back to Europe, she no longer combed lice from my hair. It was no use—we were all covered with lice, fleas, bugs. And yet, each was secretive about having lice. "You didn't want anyone to know," Oscar said. "They might think you had bad hygiene and stay away from you."

After another 1,800 kilometers northwest, the train reached the city of Aktobe, at the border of Kazakhstan and Russia. Then the train turned west in an uneven line, sometimes in Russia, other times in Kazakhstan. I imagine that, as the train cut through wooded steppe, the air outside our boxcar was fresher, with leafy green trees and rich, dark earth. We approached more populated areas. Our train crossed the Ural River at the city of Uralsk and, days later, we reached the Volga River.

With more people searching for food at each stop, we had even less to eat than before, according to Oskar. Our conversation focused on food. The older couple in our boxcar argued constantly with us and between themselves, and even in my family, my uncles, cousins, and parents disagreed: Should we use our last few resources to trade for food at the next siding or wait until the train gets to the city? Should we eat what we have now or save some bread for later? Should the children get more because they are growing, less because they are smaller, or the same as the adults? Hunger made everyone shrill—and reckless.

One day, our train was moving slowly, a few kilometers per hour. From the window, David saw a field of potatoes. He jumped off the train, dug up some potatoes, grabbed a few cabbages, ran back and clambered aboard. My mother was flailing her arms and screaming the entire time, certain he'd be left behind. Tulek was cursing even after David returned.

For as long as I can remember, even after we were safe, my mother would divide all available food among everyone and give herself the smallest portion. Then, while the others ate, my mother watched me. After I finished my portion, she offered me hers. She never ate until she was satisfied that I would eat no more, and then she'd take only a tentative bite, watching me all the time, willing herself to stop if she saw any sign that I would eat more.

Maybe it was on this journey that my mother grew even thinner. Her ears began to stick out. Two deep ridges formed between her eyes. Her voice took on a tinny and hollow quality.

But we reached the Volga, the river called Mother Volga in Russian folklore. The river, central to Russian economy, carried more than half of all river freight, provided much of the country's water for irrigation, and supported a large population of sturgeon, the source of Russia's black caviar. It is the longest river in Europe, flowing slowly south at low elevation from northwest of Moscow to the Caspian Sea. Many battles have been fought along its banks, including Stalingrad in 1942–43, which changed the course of the war when the Soviets ultimately defeated Nazi Germany after the loss of many lives on both sides.

We were less than two hundred kilometers north of Stalingrad in the summer of 1945 when my family reached the Volga River at the city of Engels. We must have crossed the Volga to the city of Saratov via one of the longest bridges in Europe. I imagine Saratov as a city with a jumble of noisy streets, soldiers, ragged women, people going in every direction, to and from Europe, Russia, and Central Asia. I imagine the adults exchanging rumors they were now hearing about the devastation in Europe and Russia, worrying about what was ahead of them.

We might have stopped for a long time at the busy train station, my father and uncles bargaining for scarce provisions, before our train continued its laborious westward journey to and into Ukraine, now part of the Soviet sphere, retaken from defeated Nazi Germany. Across Ukraine, we would have passed the ruined city of Kharkov and pressed on to Kiev, the largest city in Ukraine, an old city and an important economic and cultural center called the "mother of cities" by the Russians. Before 1941, Kiev was home to 175 thousand Jews. We didn't yet know, coming through on our train, that all were exterminated, but we might have seen, at the station, people shouting names, asking for news, holding signs, searching, searching.

We continued past Tarnopol to Lwów, to which my father had fled in 1939, then a city with 150 thousand Jews. Now, only a handful.

Near Lwów we had to change trains because the Russian train track system operated on a five-foot gauge, slightly wider than the

4.85 gauge used in Poland and much of the rest of the world. Now we boarded a passenger train, no longer a freight train. It was crowded with people standing in the aisles, sitting on the floor, even on the steps with their legs dangling out. No one in our group talked much anymore but, like my father, remained deep in thought as the train moved westward to Kraków. To home. So we thought.

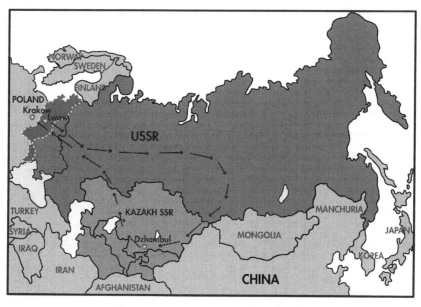

The approximate route of my family.

Belz . . . Mayn shtetle Belz,
Mayn heymele dort
Vu ich hob mayne kindersche yorn farbracht.
Zayt ihr a mol geveyn in Belz.
Mayn shtetele Belz,
Mayn heymele dort
Vu ich hob mayne kindersche yorn farbracht.

Belz . . . my village Belz,
My home there
Where I passed my childhood years.
Have you ever been to Belz
My village Belz,
My home there
Where I passed my childhood years.

"Mayn Shtetele Belz,"
Yiddish song

13

Poland, 1945

IN EARLY 1945, SOVIET forces advanced from east to west through Poland, pushing back the Nazi army, while American forces advanced from the west. The two armies met at the Elba River in Germany. Germany was cut in two. On May 8, Germany surrendered. Most of eastern Germany and areas to its east fell to the Soviets, the west to the Allies. Poland, to the east, was under Soviet control as my family struggled back.

"As we got closer to Kraków, we let the train go," my father explained. "We did not need the train anymore, because we came to our home territories. We split up, all those people from Kazakhstan; not everyone had the same idea."

My family went to Kraków. "This was my city," my father said. "I knew the people. I went to school there."

In Kraków, people gave us food, a place to stay, information, money. But we didn't stay.

"There was nothing to wait for," my father continued. " I knew one thing. I did not want to stay in Poland. Everything was different. Communism was too big. They begged me to stay; I should take some state position, as a judge, counselor, lawyer, administrator, anything, just to stay there. One man who was transferring me on a train, a *natchalnik*, said I should work with him; it was good, he said.

"I didn't want to stay.

"There were no Jews."

Only a few had survived, in hiding or in camps, and they, like us, were now trickling in, returning from their nightmares. My father met colleagues from university, but no Jews. "I saw nobody of my people." In Kraków, sixty thousand Jews had thrived before the war. Other communities were equally decimated.

Tulek went by train to Jasło, from where he, Henek, and my mother, Rózia, had fled just six years earlier, a lifetime ago. Jasło was in ruins, burned to the ground. No Jews. Tulek came back and told us no one was left. No one from my mother's family.

In Nowy Sącz, no one was left from my father's family.

Mothers, fathers, sisters, brothers, aunts, uncles, cousins, friends. No one.

In the Soviet Union, my family had received little news about the Holocaust in Europe. At the start of our long journey, my family hoped, now that the war was over, they could go home. But they found no home. Added to the shock and devastation were rumors that in some parts of Poland, Poles continued to carry out pogroms against the few returning Jews. "Why are you people still alive?" they'd ask.

My family was afraid to stay.

My father decided we had to leave: "It was the end of the war, but not the end of our journey. We had to go away, from Poland, from Europe."

Eli, Eli
Shelo yigamer leolam
Ḥakhol vehayam
Rishrush shet hamayim
Verak hashamayin
T'filat ha'adam

Lord, Lord
I pray that these things never end
The sand and the sea
The rush of the waters
The crash of the heavens
The prayers of man.

"Eli, Eli," by Hannah Senesh,
Hungarian Jew and resistance
fighter during World War II;
now part of Hebrew liturgy

14

꧁꧂

Borders

To leave, we would have to cross two borders: from Soviet-controlled Poland to the country of Czechoslovakia, which was also under Soviet control, and from Czechoslovakia to Austria. Austria, under Allied control, would be our gateway to somewhere, we didn't yet know where. We knew only that we couldn't stay.

Once again, we set forth on a journey we were not permitted to take. The Soviets restricted all travel, and particularly monitored the borders.

At the train station in Kraków, we boarded a passenger train, old, dusty, crowded, and lumbering, but thankfully not a boxcar, for a trip of 250 kilometers south to Kudowa-Zdrój, on the border between Poland and Czechoslovakia, a gathering place for refugees.

On the Polish side of the border, we were housed in a refugee camp as my father and others planned the next part of our escape. After about four weeks, we organized into small groups; we would sneak across the border on foot. My parents and I, with two others, were in one group. Tulek, Oskar, Selma, and a fourth person were in another group. Henek and David were with others.

On this part of our odyssey, leaving the refugee camp in Kudowa-Zdrój or in the woods, my father lost his rucksack, the bag that carried his papers showing he had completed law studies at the University Jagiellonian, the bag he had carried biking to Lwów, walking to Tarnopol, in the boxcar to Siberia, in the barrack, on the freight train of escape from Siberia, in Dzhambul, on the train across Kazakhstan and Russia, and into Poland. He told me once, quietly, that he picked up what he thought was his rucksack but it belonged to someone else, and later returned it to the owner. But whoever carried my father's rucksack must have just dumped it in the woods when the person realized it wasn't his. The way he told me, I understood that, with the loss of his papers, my father, in his mind at least, lost his profession.

That crossing, walking stealthily through the forests and hills of the border between Poland and Czechoslovakia, when I was almost four, is my first clear memory, not filtered by the recollection of others.

I'm with a group, my mother, father, and several others, traveling on foot, day, night, climbing up and down small hills. My father is carrying me on his strong shoulders. Everyone is very quiet.

"Tatuś," I call from my perch astride my father's shoulders. "Sama, sama!" Myself! I'm a big girl, and I don't want to be carried! My father's hand pats my leg, "Shhh." But I am persistent: "Sama!" At last, he reaches up, lifts me off his shoulders and, with one more "Shh," stands me on the hillside. Proudly I start climbing uphill, grabbing small bushes and branches to hoist my way up. I'm almost at the top! I can do it! I reach for a shrub and, suddenly, surprisingly, out comes the plant, roots and all, and I'm hurtled backward, rolling sideways like a log, all the way to the bottom of the long hill. I howl at the humiliation. I failed. I have not proven I'm a big girl. My father and mother rush down the hill. "I'm not hurt!" I shout, mistaking the alarm in their eyes, and cry even louder. The more they try to calm me, the more I cry. Finally, exhausted, I sniff quietly against my father's chest, and then his strong arms lift me back onto his shoulders.

In this way, we continue. After a long day and night of climbing, eating only food we can forage, we come to our destination: a small cabin in the woods, a way station set up by the Beriha. The name means "flight" in Hebrew. The group was an underground network that helped surviving Jews find their way to western Europe and encouraged them to immigrate to Palestine.

My father stumbled through the door of the cabin. "This is my little girl, take care of her," he said before passing out and sleeping for days. My mother and the others were equally exhausted.

Eventually, our contacts, fierce young men, some still in their teens, who had survived the Nazis as partisans in the woods, put us on a train. If we were lucky, the train would take us across the border into Austria and out of Soviet-dominated areas. But first the train had to stop at Bratislava, a Czech city close to the Austrian border, which was monitored by Soviet soldiers.

On the train to Bratislava, to our relief, we met up with Tulek, Oskar, and Selma.

"Our group got caught," Oskar told us. "We were taken to a police station in Náchod in Czechoslovakia. We were sitting there a long time, waiting when..." He paused, let out a low, small chuckle. "When a pickup truck full of shoes pulled up. Someone shouted, 'Shoes, shoes.' The police, the clerks, everyone from the police station ran to the truck." While the police were distracted, grabbing shoes, Oskar and the three others just walked out, escaped. They found their contact, who arranged travel permits and put them on the passenger train to Bratislava. David and Henek had similar close calls before they met up with us.

The Red Army was guarding the border at Bratislava. The Soviets permitted no one but Greeks to cross the border into Austria, out of Soviet domination. There was a civil war in Greece, and the Communists were fighting for control. The Soviets wanted Greeks to go back to Greece to help establish Communism there.

We were determined. We had to cross that border.

15

Bratislava, 1945

"Years later, I still can't get it out of my mind," Oskar tells me on the telephone from his home in California. I have called to wish him a happy birthday. We always speak in October; his birthday is October 1 and mine is October 18. His American name is Joe, but I still call him Oskar. He calls me Anusia, my childhood name.

"I think of you every day," he says. "You know, that time when you saved all of our lives. You were so little, not yet four years old."

I've heard the story since I was a child. It was always retold when the family got together.

Before starting our risky escape, in the refugee camp at the Polish border, my family huddled and discussed the plan to cross Czechoslovakia and escape across the border into Austria. In the dark room, my mother held me close.

"*Ret Yiddish. Das kind zol nicht farshtein,*" she said softly, telling the others to speak Yiddish so I wouldn't understand. I heard her words but I knew my family couldn't keep secrets from me. I understood all their languages.

"So much confusion," my father started. "Soldiers leaving the front; people trying to get home. That's our opportunity."

"Ah, Stalin will never let us leave," Henek interrupted. "We're prisoners! We're Polish and they control Poland. We've lived in Russia; the Soviets own us."

"That's right; we'll have to prove we've never been there at all."

"Ach, how will we do that?" my mother asked. "Look, we speak Polish. We speak Russian. How can we prove we don't belong?"

"The Beriha has a suggestion," my father answered, and I recognized the name of the underground network helping Jews. "We make up a story. We got lost. We're Greek; we fled and, in the turmoil, we stumbled across the border into Soviet-controlled areas. We didn't see the checkpoint towers. Somehow the guards missed us. Later we realized we were on the wrong side. We don't belong and now we're trying to get back to our homeland."

Tulek: "One problem with the plan, Mundek: we don't speak Greek."

Henek: "Greek, shmeek. We might as well try speaking Hebrew."

Tulek perked up: "Hebrew! I bet it's Greek to the Russians."

"That's the idea," my father encouraged.

"Hebrew. We studied enough of it. *Ani medaberet, atoh daberah.*" My mother recited her childhood declensions. "I'm willing to try."

"Good. Here's what we'll do," my father explained. "I'll be the spokesman. I'll say I studied Russian in school. Everyone else will speak only Hebrew. No matter what they ask, no matter how scared, you don't answer, and the only sound out of your mouth is Hebrew. Do you understand?"

Everyone nodded solemnly.

"But the child?" someone asked.

"I'll take care of her," said my mother.

"She'll understand," said Tulek, always my champion. And I knew I was important.

In a few days, we were on a train toward Austria and freedom. We arrived at the check point in Bratislava. Soviet soldiers searched every train.

When they came to Henek, he was ready.

"You," a Soviet soldier said, pointing to Henek, "speak Greek!"

"*Shema Yisroel adonoi eloheinu adonoi echod. Boruch sheim kvod malchuso leolom voed. Veohafto et adonoi...*" The ancient Hebrew words said at the beginning of every prayer.

The soldiers stomped toward us. I peeked out from my mother's side.

The big men stopped.

"Papers!" demanded the one in front.

My father handed over a paper purporting to be a document stating that we were Greek refugees.

"Greeks, huh?" The soldier looked us over.

A soldier in the back shuffled his feet, opened his mouth, then closed it.

"Hm," the one in front pondered, "Greek." Suddenly he turned to me. "The child!" he exclaimed, reaching for me.

My mother was perfectly still. The index finger of her right hand rested lightly on the side of her mouth. A vein pulsed on her forehead.

"*Nyet,*" my father said. "She's a small child. What will you have with her? Take me."

"You?" The soldier looked sternly at my father. "I want to interrogate the child. She'll tell us the truth."

The soldier picked me up. He was even bigger than my father. His uniform was scratchy and the brim of his cap was close to my face. His teeth were brown as he smiled at me.

"You're a nice little girl," he said, carrying me out of the train. And, in a conversational tone: "*Ponimayit po russki?*" Do you speak Russian?

Over the big man's shoulder, I looked back at my mother as I was carried to the door of the train. Her eyes were round as she looked at me; one hand covered her mouth. My father stood up to follow, but other soldiers blocked his way. He, too, had his hand over his mouth.

The big soldier carried me out of the train into a small room in a nearby wooden structure. Two more soldiers stood at attention at each end of the room, and two chairs had been placed in the middle.

The soldier put me down on one chair and sat opposite.

"What's your name?" he asked in Russian, which I perfectly understood.

I sat still.

"I bet you have a pretty name. I'll play a game with you. If I'm wrong, say 'nyet' and you win, and if I'm right say 'da' and I win. Is your name Natasha? Maybe its Anna?"

I sat in silence.

"You must be tired. You've been on the train a long time, haven't you. Where are you from?"

Silence.

"Are you Greek? You can say 'da' and I'll let you go."

Silence.

"Do you have a doll? I bet you'd like a doll with a pretty blue dress. What do you think?"

My stomach rumbled.

"Ah, I bet you're hungry," my interrogator continued. "I'll have some bread and butter brought in, and maybe some pieroshki with smetana. I bet you'd like that, wouldn't you?"

Silence.

He took something out of his pocket. "Would you like an apple?" He reached out his hand, offering me the succulent treat.

I looked at it. My mouth watered. Finally, I opened my mouth.

"Mama," I said.

He held the apple. He continued interrogating, I don't know for how long. I never wavered. The only word I uttered was "Mama."

At the end, the large soldier put the apple back in his pocket, picked me up, and marched me back to my family. Handing me to my father, he said:

"She doesn't know Russian. You can go."

℘

"You were gone about thirty minutes," Oskar says. "We were really worried. We thought our goose was cooked. We could have been sent back to Siberia or worse. But you never said a thing. You never let on.

"After the Russian soldiers interrogated you, after you came back, you told your mom and dad, very proudly: '*Ja im nic niepowiedziałam.*' 'I didn't tell them anything.'

"You saved us. I'll never forget it."

16

The Transom

OUR TRAIN CROSSED THE border into Austria and at last we were out of Soviet-controlled areas. We no longer had to pretend to be Greek, but we were outside of any legal system. We didn't know where we would go. All of the countries of Europe and most of the countries of the world had rules on immigration. The Beriha was the first to help us. Now in the Allied zone we would be helped by the American Red Cross and the newly formed United Nations Relief and Rehabilitation Administration, known as UNRRA.

We arrived in Vienna, a center for processing persons displaced by the war. Once there, we were taken to a hospital to be examined, cleaned up, and deloused. The process took an entire day. Our clothes were heated to kill the bugs, and we were covered with powder, DDT.

After that, we wanted to be classified as displaced persons by the western Allies because that would permit us to remain in the Allied-controlled areas of Europe. Anywhere would be better than Poland or the Soviet Union, we felt.

But our situation and desire to resettle was complicated by the fact that, at the end of 1945, large numbers of refugees were streaming into the Allied zones. The processing of displaced persons was chaotic and lengthy, the criteria confusing and still developing. Many countries argued for repatriation of their postwar refugees, regardless of the wishes of the refugees. The situation of displaced Jews was of particular concern. The western Allies recognized that Jews could not be repatriated to their countries of origin because of the severe persecution and near genocide of Jews and because anti-Semitism was still prevalent in many of those countries.

The issue of repatriation was not fully settled at the time my family sought classification as displaced persons. The Soviets, in particular, urged repatriation of a broad range of persons and made no exceptions for Jews. My family had been in the Soviet Union, albeit against our will, and we feared being forced to return. My family's fear focused especially on me because I was born in Soviet-controlled Kazakhstan. This fear came to dominate my mother's thoughts even years later when I was an adult. She feared people would find out where I was born, and she often told me: "Don't ever go there. They'll think you're one of theirs and want to keep you."

Because of our fear of being sent back to the Soviet Union, my family approached the classification process as displaced persons carefully. We emphasized that we were Polish Jews, and we were concerned that a long delay would make it more likely that we would be detained and returned to the Soviet Union.

In Vienna, we were sent to a hall filled with refugees seeking to obtain papers, people anxious, crying, talking, shouting. Tulek looked around. There were hundreds, maybe thousands, waiting to be processed. How could we be taken more quickly? A door at the far end led to another room, where sympathetic but overworked officials sat interrogating refugees and making decisions about who would be sent where. Above the door was a transom, and it was open twelve inches.

Tulek quickly gathered together our few identifying documents and tied them into a small bundle. My father urged restraint, wait our turn, but Tulek pushed his way through the crowd as close to the door as he could get. Then, with all his might, he threw our papers through the transom. It was a huge risk; everything could have been lost.

Fortunately, the bundle landed on the floor near the desk of a person in charge. He picked them up, leafed through them, and, "Who are these people?" he asked. "Let them come through."

We were called into the room. We were processed as displaced persons.

≈

After that, the Beriha took us, by open truck, to a refugee camp in Salzburg. On the way, they took us to view Berchtesgaden. We, my parents, uncles, cousins, me—we were there. We saw Hitler's summer retreat. Hitler was defeated. We had survived.

My father: "We stayed in Salzburg for a while, but we weren't comfortable. We couldn't stay there. We felt it was too anti-Semitic.

"This was in the fall of 1945. I remember it, the weather was such a terrible weather, windy and rainy. I had a few colleagues, other survivors who had arrived earlier, friends, who now reached out to me. One or two were in Salzburg, others in Munich and in Bamberg, in Bayern. My colleagues asked me to work with them. They told me not many educated Jews were left, not many survived. They wanted me to come with them and work with them in a displaced persons camp. I said okay."

My father's records show we were in the Anreuth transit camp in December 1945 and January 1946, and then, at the end of January, we were moved to the displaced persons camp in Fürth bei Nuremberg in Germany. My father worked there with the Jewish organizations. He helped build a Jewish court.

Ich weiß nicht, was soll es bedeuten
Daß ich so traurig bin
Ein Maerchen aus alten Zeiten,
Das kommt mir nicht aus dem Sinn.
Die Luft ist Kuhl, und es dunkelt
Und ruhig fließt der Rhein.
Der Gipfel des Berges funkelt
Im Abendsonnenschein.

I don't know what is the reason
That I am so full of sorrow;
A fable from times long past
Will not allow me to rest.
The air is cool in the twilight
And gently flows the Rhine;
The mountain top is gleaming
In fading rays of sunshine.

from "Die Lorelei," by Heinrich
Heine (1797–1856)

17

❧❧

Displaced Persons

BY 1946, WHEN MY family arrived in Germany, there were about 180 thousand Jewish displaced persons, called DPs, in Germany. The DP camp in Fürth where we were taken was one of a number of such centers established by the Allies in Germany to house those uprooted by the war, both Jews and non-Jews. Fürth was a small camp, established later than others, and held about a thousand persons when we were there, all Jews.

We weren't required to live in the camp, but we had no place else to go. Adults had no jobs; we'd lost our homes; and every country had limitations on immigration, quotas, or other restrictive requirements.

The camp was created by removing locals from existing buildings and surrounding the area with a high barbed-wire fence. When we lived there, and after my childhood of not being permitted to leave places unless we fled, always fearfully, I believed the fence was there to keep us inside. Years later, I learned that the barbed-wire fence was intended to keep us safe from people on the outside, some of whom still harbored us ill will. In fact, residents of the camp were free to come and go, and my parents and others frequently walked to the town of Fürth. From there they could take the train to Nuremberg, five kilometers away, or to other communities. For most trips outside of the camp, though, we were transported in open trucks.

A small guardhouse, manned by one or two American soldiers, stood at the entrance to the camp, and we checked in upon entering or leaving. A long street of gravel extended from the guardhouse through the camp to another, much smaller street at the far end, as if forming a long letter T.

*My mother, father. and me in Fürth. The entrance
and guard house are behind us.*

Midway down the main street, a small monument, erected shortly after we arrived, was a memorial to those lost in the war, many of whose fates remained unknown. It looked not unlike a large grave, constructed of a gray marble base surrounded by a chain fence and a headstone carved with the Star of David and Hebrew lettering.

At the memorial for Jews killed in the Holocaust.

In my memory, as you entered the camp from the guardhouse, to the right stood the administration building, larger than most of the other buildings. This was where my father worked, I was proud to point out. To the left was the synagogue, a smaller pine structure, and beyond it, abutting the barbed-wire fence, stood a two-room school-house. Several grades were taught in each room, equipped with rows of desks and chairs; younger children sat on one side, older children on the other. In front of the school was a recreational field, with swings at one end and a small hill at the other.

*Schoolchildren in Fürth. I'm seated second from right in the front,
a white bow in my hair.*

A small rivulet or canal ran just outside the barbed-wire fence behind the schoolhouse and along that side of the camp, separating the camp further from the outside world. My favorite memory is of tall yellow sunflowers that grew near the school, a surprising burst of color in the otherwise brown fields and gray buildings. I can still see their sturdy stalks backing against the wire fence, their large yellow faces with round dark centers like eyes, looking up at the indestructible sky.

Our residences, two-story nondescript gray structures, lined the two streets of the camp. Each building housed about a dozen families. Behind the building where my family lived, the weed-filled yard held a rusty manual merry-go-round. I liked to sit on its small wooden bench next to my friend Gizia, our eyes closed to the glare of the sun, while Gizia's mother turned the wheel that propelled us round and round.

In the spring, patches of wild strawberries appeared in the yard, and we searched for the small fruit where it grew hidden underneath jagged leaves, squatting when we saw a glint of scarlet, picking carefully, and scooping the berries into our mouths, savoring their tart-sweet juiciness.

We were in the first residential building on the right, past the administration buildings. My mother, father, Tulek, and I shared one room. A potbellied stove stood in the middle of the room, providing heat. I slept in a double bed with my parents, in the middle, a warm and cozy place. To one side, my father slept on his back with his right arm flung over his eyes. My mother lay very still on her left side with her face away from the center of the bed. Whenever I looked over her shoulder, her eyes were open. On a single bed at the other end of the room slept Tulek, but he frequently came in late at night after we were asleep.

We shared a kitchen at one end of the hall, and an indoor bathroom at the other end, with three other families. We cooperated with the other families on the shared facilities, which seemed luxurious to us.

UNNRA and a welfare agency called "Joint," the American Jewish Joint Distribution Committee, provided necessities: bread, sardines, evaporated milk, liverwurst if we were lucky, other canned or powdered food, and some clothes. We were able to supplement these with additional items Tulek got on the black market in Fürth or in the larger city of Nuremberg. Later, we received packages from my mother's cousins in America.

I felt special. I had three daddies: my father, kind and handsome, who took me by the hand on his important missions; Tulek, who made me laugh and brought me presents from the black market; and Henek, who teased me and brought news of the world outside the DP camp.

I felt important. I knew everyone and had many friends, with whom I ran up and down the street, swung on the swings in the playground, or made snowmen in the winter.

I felt privileged. We received packages from cousins in America and I always had a warm sweater.

My cousin Harry, grandson of Rubin Ferziger, the youngster who stayed in the United States in the 1890s when my great grandmother took the rest of the family back to Poland, remembers sending those packages from Texas.

"Mama had big boxes in the kitchen and dining room. I helped," Harry told me, "the way a child would. I would put things in and take them out."

"What did your mother send?"

"Cigarettes, lots of cigarettes. They were good for their exchange value, easy to barter and better than cash. Also coffee, sugar, flour, clothing. Mama packed carefully so nothing would break, putting clothes between things."

Tulek traded cigarettes on the *schwarzmarkt*, the black market. All the men, and many of the women, smoked. The cigarettes my uncles smoked in Fürth were a great improvement over the cigarettes they'd smoked in Kazakhstan: tobacco which they hand-rolled in newspaper or any other available paper.

On Saturdays, American soldiers would drive an open truck into the camp. American soldiers were unlike other soldiers I had seen. These solders smiled and we were not frightened of them. When the truck entered the camp, we children would run to line up and wait as the Americans gave each of us an orange and a chocolate bar. The first black man I ever saw was an American soldier with a moon-shaped face who smiled broadly, showing even, white teeth, as he handed me these gifts. I took the special things home, and my mother or father would peel the orange, which we would all share, liquid spilling down my chin as I savored the bite and sweetness of the juice. The chocolate bar didn't get shared, however; it was understood that this treat was all mine. I'd break off a small square and put it in my mouth where it would stick before melting, the texture like silk down my throat, the taste as sweet as sugar but with a slight bitterness and hints of milk and butter. I had never tasted anything so beguiling. I was quick to dart for the truck on those Saturdays when it came into the camp.

❧

I was surprised by all the photographers. I handed General Eisenhower a bouquet of purple and rust fall flowers, slightly wilted in my clutch.

"*Shalom*," I said, as I'd been coached.

The General bent his long frame down and offered a warm smile. The photographs capture the well-known face and, next to him, a blonde child, about five years old, with large, solemn eyes—the color of beer, my uncle Tulek said—and a thin smile. My warm sweater is slightly puckered at one shoulder under a dark skirt with suspenders.

General Dwight David Eisenhower had come to visit the displaced persons camp in Fürth in the fall of 1946. My father worked in the camp's office as an administrator, a representative of the refugees. He was employed by the UNRRA, the organization that took care of the DPs, and helped the US army in operating the camp. It seemed to me my father had a very important job. Because of my father's position, I was asked to present flowers to visiting dignitaries. I was proud each time I did my task.

General Eisenhower is at left. I'm the blonde standing next to him. Gizia Blachowa is my friend, and the boy in front is Heniu Sherman.

*General Eisenhower is at left. I'm the blonde
with my friend Gizia.*

I'm meeting General Clay.

In school, where I started kindergarten, classes were conducted in Yiddish. One day, one of my classmates, a girl about my age, became ill and was taken by the American soldiers to the hospital in Nuremberg. When she came back a few weeks later, she'd learned an American song the soldiers taught her, "You Are My Sunshine." We memorized the song and sang it carefully, even though we didn't understand the words. In my mind, this American song of sunshine was like the bright yellow sunflowers growing behind the school— and hinted of the golden land where there would be no rubble, plenty of everything, and where even soldiers smiled.

Still grieving for his lost wife and his small son, Iziu, Henek continued to search for anyone who might know them, who had seen them, who could tell him where they were, if they were alive. He wrote letters, posted notices. Finally, one day he had a response. A man from Jasło had seen them in their last days in a concentration camp in Poland. Henek's wife and child were dead.

18

❧❧

Henek Marries Again

ERNA WAS THE FIRST woman I had ever seen wearing lipstick. I thought she was beautiful. She had no lines on her forehead or between her eyes, like my mother or the other women. Her hair fell in waves from a big sausage curl on top of her head. She was rounder than most other adults, who were pale and thin, and her skin was soft. I still remember her dress: dark grey wool, long sleeves, round neck, with a wide black leather belt and an A-line knee-length skirt. She wore knee-high black leather boots.

My uncle Henek met Erna in a nearby town where he worked. There wasn't much work inside the DP camp. My father worked in the office; Tulek traded on the black market; but Henek, a printer, left the camp and found a job as a printer at a newspaper in Regensburg. Erna worked at that newspaper as a "photo reporter."

Erna visited us at the DP camp and always came with a camera. To me, the camera seemed to be from another world. No one I knew had a camera. She stood in front of us, tracking adjustments and turning dials. She brought gadgets, too, the "latest thing." One day she held out her arm—she wore a watch with a second hand. I watched it ticking around the dial. Another day, she showed me a kaleidoscope, how to hold it up to one eye and turn. I watched in awe as brilliant colors of blue, green, red, and yellow fell into intricate beautiful patterns.

On another visit, as we were waiting in the train station for her train back to Regensburg, Erna opened her purse and took out a banana. I had never seen one! I stared at the strange fruit. Erna showed me how to peel its thick skin. I took a small tentative bite, surprised at its exotic taste. After that banana, I was hers.

Erna came from Bielsko-Biała, a small city near the Polish border with Germany, where her father started the first coffee-roasting company in Poland. After the Nazis invaded Poland, Erna and her family, like my mother and father and many others, fled east to Lwów. Erna's family arrived later than my parents and were not taken by the Soviets but remained in the city until the Nazis attacked the Soviet Union and took Lwów. After that, Erna's family was forced to move into the Jewish ghetto there.

One day, returning home after running an errand for her mother, Erna saw a Nazi truck parked in front of the building where her family lived. Inside the open back of the truck she saw her mother. As Erna stood staring transfixed, her mother made a small motion with her hand as if pushing Erna off. She backed to another street and fled. She never saw her mother and two brothers again.

Her father she saw only once more, that same night. He told her he had arranged a job for her in Kraków and gave her papers he had bought proving she was Aryan. She left by train the next day.

Erna was eighteen, fluent in Polish and German, with pale blue eyes and false Aryan papers that gave her name as "Irka." Shortly after she started at the job her father had arranged in Kraków, the place of work was raided by the Nazis; luckily she was away and was not caught. Erna then moved to the resort town of Zakopane where she found work, first as a German-Polish translator for a soldier in the Gestapo, and later as a maid in a house where Gestapo soldiers lived. While washing dishes at a sink, she later recalled, soldiers and visitors talked in the room directly behind her work space. She was careful to keep her back to the room so no visitor would see her face. For three years, Erna survived, fleeing from one place to another when she thought someone might suspect she was a Jew, finding whatever work she could.

By the end of the war, circumstances brought Erna to Regensburg. Having survived as an Aryan and not seeing another Jew for many years, Erna thought she was the only Jew still alive in the world.

Then she met my uncle Henek. He was a widower of thirty-nine; Erna was twenty-four. They were married in April, 1947. My parents and Tulek attended the small ceremony in Regensburg.

After their marriage, I overheard Tulek talking to my mother. "There are rumors," he said. "Erna married Henek to get a ticket to the United States. You'll see. She'll leave him right after we get there."

It was no secret that Erna wanted to go to the United States. And everyone knew that my family was on the list to immigrate. We were lucky. We had sponsors in the United States who would vouch for us, agree to take care of us financially. It was only a matter of time before we would leave the DP camp.

From left to right, Tulek, Erna, Henek, my mother, and my father in the DP camp in Fürth.

19

∾⫷∿⫸∾

Our Life in Fürth

I N FÜRTH, TULEK MADE frequent train trips to bombed-out Nuremberg to trade on the black market. I was the envy of my friends, as Tulek brought back wonderful presents. That first winter, he found a navy blue army uniform, which my mother cut and stitched into a warm snowsuit for me, with a belted jacket, trousers, and cap. The following year—wonder of wonders—Tulek came back with a sled! It was made of wood with metal runners, and large enough to seat two. On snowy days, my friends and I would fly down the hill near the schoolhouse.

Just before my sixth birthday, I received a very grown-up present from Tulek: gold hoop earrings with tiny opals, my birthstone, and a matching ring. I didn't have pierced ears, so I couldn't wear the earrings. Even though the custom in Europe at that time, and in Dzhambul where I was born, was to pierce the ears of baby girls, and all the women had pierced ears, my father objected to having my ears pierced. He said he wanted his baby girl to be "perfect," with "nothing artificial piercing her body."

I begged to wear the ring for Yom Kippur, the Jewish high holy day. My mother and Tulek could never resist my pleas, so I proudly wore the ring when we went to synagogue. I stayed for a while, but then came Yizkor, the solemn memorial service for the dead. Only those who had lost a parent, spouse, child, or sibling could attend. In the synagogue, everyone was serious and sad and my family sent me out of the building. Alone, I went out the front door. At each side of the entrance stood a large urn filled with sand. Amusing myself, I dug into the sand with my hands, sifting and molding the sand into balls, squares, and primitive sandcastles. After a while, my family came out. My mother took my hand in hers.

"Where's your ring?" she asked.

I looked at my bare hand. "I don't know," I replied, and confessed that I'd been playing in the sand.

The men turned the urns upside down, the sand was carefully combed all over the ground, but the ring was never found.

Of the several dozen children in the DP camp, only about six were my age. My closest friend, Gizia, was a chubby, dark-haired girl. Heniu was called my boyfriend by the adults, and there was also Ola, blonde with a dimple in her cheek. A toddler in the camp had the same name as I, so she was called *mała Anusia*, little Anusia, and I became *duzia Anusia*, big Anusia. And I was getting bigger. Somehow, my parents arranged extra rations of milk; after two years at the camp, I had become quite sturdy.

We celebrated all the Jewish religious festivals. My favorite was Chanukah in December 1947. I was six. I took part in the pageant, flapping a hand toy made of two sticks with a puppet on strings in the middle whenever the teacher gave a signal. I wore my new, warm, hand-knit sweater, white with strips of colorful winter images of fir trees and snowmen in blue, green, and red, and leather buttons down the front.

Presents were distributed to the children, each child receiving one present from a wish list we had given the teacher. First on my list, for the second year in a row, was a doll. I watched as other children opened their presents. No one got his or her first choice, but each

I'm on the left, next to Gizia, with Ola on the right.

Chanukah celebration. I'm at back, left.

With my doll.

My mother and father in the DP camp.

child was delighted to get something. When it was my turn to open my present, with everyone watching, I unwrapped the paper—and there was a doll, about ten or twelve inches long, a bonnet covering her bald head, in a blue floral dress and wrapped in a pink blanket. Reaching further, I pulled out a wooden doll carriage painted pink and green. I was in heaven. After that, I walked around camp with my friends, pushing that carriage, a small, proud smile on my face.

In addition to religious festivals, the people in the camp held many social events: children's birthdays, family milestones, meetings, parties, and dances. I loved dancing with my father, his right arm around my waist, his left hand holding mine, as we twirled around to the one-two-three, one-two-three of a Viennese waltz. I danced with Tulek, too, his favorite dancing partner, he told me, while his girlfriend of the moment had to wait on the side.

I remember attending a costume ball with my mother, father, and Tulek. We were not dressed in costume but in our finest clothes: the men in suits, my mother in a narrow dress flaring into a trumpet hem, and me in a short blue dress, received in a carton from America. I was intrigued by those in costume. I'd never seen people dressed with such deliberation. The costumes worn by two women particularly attracted me, and the adults around me commented about their risqué attire: one in an evening gown, and the other in tails and a top hat with a painted moustache. Tulek danced with each of the women and was with them when a photographer took their photo as I watched proudly. Tulek danced with many other women, too. That night, he met the Pogorelsky sisters. Doba, the taller, younger one at twenty-three, was a lively and loquacious blonde; Riva, twenty-five, was smaller, a quiet, pretty brunette. The sisters, fifteen and seventeen when the war started, had hidden in the woods of eastern Poland, joined a band of partisans, carried rifles, slept on the ground covered with leaves and snow; some of their band had literally frozen to death.

"Women like Tulek," my mother told me. And, after the war, survivors were eager to marry and get on with a "normal" life. But Tulek was in no hurry. No matter how many women he met, he wouldn't marry; he wanted to wait until we came to America.

⌇

The War Crimes Trials had begun in Nuremberg, five kilometers from Fürth, in November 1945. After we arrived, my father was designated an official observer at the Nuremberg trials on behalf of the refugees from our camp. Mundek spoke fluent German, Polish, and Russian, and he would report back to the camp about the progress of the trials.

Many mornings, my father would dress in a suit and tie and climb into the back of an open pickup truck with several other men. He returned late at night. One afternoon, we were told there had been an accident and the truck had turned over. We waited anxiously for several days until my father arrived home, a white bandage wrapped around his head. He visited the hospital in Nuremberg a few times after that to have the bandage changed. On one of the visits he took me. I was five.

The hospital was an imposing building of white stone, five stories high. Inside, there were two elevator shafts, each with a row of open elevator cabins, like a dumbwaiter, one row continuously moving up and the other continuously moving down. You'd stand before the shaft of the elevator moving up, and, as an open cabin came even with the floor, you were supposed to jump on. This day, my father stepped onto the moving cabin, but I stood, frozen.

There I was, outside two open elevator shafts. Quickly, a doctor and a nurse appeared at my side, one standing close on each side of me. They were German. They never said a word to me, but they stood still for as long as it took my father to make his way back to me.

This time, my father lifted me in his arms, and we jumped on the elevator together.

⌇

Whenever the refugees at the camp gathered, talk centered

around how they had survived. Some were pale and weak; others had crude blue tattoos on their arms. Everyone was somber. Each story was unique, but everyone would express disbelief—had they really made it?

"How did I get through?" "Why did I survive when my loved ones didn't?"

My mother, too, would repeat her story, wracked with guilt: how she left her mother and sister and thus survived—explaining, over and over, how her mother and sister had insisted she go to look for Mundek; how her mother was too fragile to flee and her older sister, Ita, was determined to stay. "Ita told me I had to go," my mother would chant.

Years later, when I was a teenager, I asked my mother the familiar question: "How can you believe in God, with all that has happened?"

"I have to believe!"

"Why?"

"I have to believe because I survived and they didn't."

Those who survived were desperate to learn the fate of those who were "lost" or "disappeared." They continued to hope families could be found, loved ones would be alive. Continued to think there was something they could do, if only they tried hard enough.

They networked frantically. They posted messages on bulletin boards, on walls, in newspapers. Letters were dispatched, crossed, forwarded from one to another: "Did you know...? Have you heard...? Did you see...?" As long as there were no witnesses, there could be hope. Yet they longed for witnesses.

Slowly, information filtered in.

My mother's sister, Ita, had been taken to a concentration camp in central Poland and killed there. Her mother, Debora, survived in Jasło until almost the end of the war, hidden in the home of a neighbor, in their crawl space. Late in 1944, believing it was safe, Debora left the house and walked toward the rynek. Someone recognized her and pointed her out to Nazi soldiers, and she was shot in the street.

After a year of letter writing, my father discovered that his brother Sine had been killed in a Nazi "street action." It happened in 1944 in Podwołoczysk in Ukraine. My father thought he had saved Sine when he shouted to him not to get on the boxcar that took my father to Siberia.

My father's mother, Sala, had also been murdered. During the winter of 1941, the Nazis prepared for a winter siege in Russia and confiscated all furs. In Nowy Sącz, a neighbor denounced Sala as the widow of a furrier and a Jew. Sala was rounded up, taken to the bridge that separated the town from the Jewish cemetery, and shot, along with several others.

But still my father knew nothing about his brother Józek and his half-brother, Albert. During the first year of our stay in the camp, my father received a letter, postmarked July 4, 1946, from his family's hometown of Nowy Sącz: "*Kohany Mundku*," the letter read. "Dear Mundek, I received your letter addressed to your brother Józek and as I work for the Jewish Board, I want to report to you that unfortunately so far none of your family members reported to Nowy Sącz and we don't know anything regarding their whereabouts. Warm greetings for you as well as your wife and child."

My father continued searching and writing letters.

20

Józek

I MET MY UNCLE Józek for the first time in 1968, when I visited him at his home in Grenoble, where he and his wife, Claire, lived at the time. He was a tall, handsome man, bigger and fuller than my father, with a proud bearing. We spoke Polish. "*Wujek*," Uncle, I called him, not addressing him directly as you do in English but speaking formally in the third person.

"Call me *ty*," you, he urged me.

"I can't, I never learned it. I was a little girl when I spoke Polish and I only talked to my elders."

As Józek drove me around the southern French countryside in his gray Citroen, he spoke of his life during the war: "After I left Poland in 1937, I lived with our half-brother, Albert, in Paris. I was able to enroll in medical school at the Sorbonne. I had been in the Polish army before I went to university. I was called back into service when invasion was imminent. I returned."

"What? You went back?"

"Yes. To rejoin the army. What happened after, well, I was sent to Hungary. I was captured by the Nazis but managed to escape and made my way south. I got on a ship to Marseilles. Once in France, I connected with the Resistance."

I concentrated hard, focusing on Polish words unfamiliar to me. We drove along a country road outside of Grenoble, the early May sunshine playing among the trees outside the car window. Józek, his hand in a brown leather driving glove, gestured out the window. "Here's where my colleague fell...We hid in those woods...I fled to this village.

"Claire saved me."

Claire was a young French Catholic woman who hid him from the Nazis. Eventually they married.

℘

Józek died in 2003. A few weeks later, I traveled to France to pay my respects. I stood at the stone base of his grave, glanced at the column, then looked up to the cross on top.

"We buried Grandpapa in Grand-mère's family tomb," Józek's granddaughter explained. "The priest understood about Grandpapa. We held a small prayer service, no mass. The night before the funeral, we had a rabbi who recited," she paused, "Kaddish?"

Later, I sat on the floor of the dining room of Józek's apartment in Grenoble as Józek's son opened the carved doors of a mahogany sideboard and pulled out cardboard boxes and folders. Silently, he handed me a brown folder, neatly tied with string. It was labeled "Mundek." Carefully I untied the string and opened the stiff cover. Inside were letters, their envelopes yellow and brittle to the touch. They released a musty smell. I focused on my father's handwriting and the envelopes addressed to Józek.

I lifted one, held it to my mouth.

℘

December 19, 1946: "*Kohany bracie Józku!*" I read, Dear brother Józek! "...we found each other and we got used to thinking that we are alive and that one brother has another..."

The brothers found each other when one of the many letters my father wrote, searching for any surviving family, found its way to the gimnazjum in Nowy Sącz at the same time as a similar letter from Józek. At the time, Józek lived in the village of Vizille in the south of France, with Claire and their two sons. A daughter and another son would soon follow.

In a photo of my uncle Józek, he's a tall man in a double-breasted suit, sad-faced but movie star handsome, with full dark hair parted in the middle. He's seated next to a petite, black-haired woman. Each holds a small boy, one dark, the other fair: my cousins.

"Real cousins, my Anusia, my daughter, says of your sons..." Mundek wrote Józek about me. "Anusia is bragging that she has real cousins. Even children understand how difficult it is nowadays."

From Józek my father learned the fate of their half-brother, Albert Löw. Józek sent a photo of Albert, dark and good-looking, with smooth hair, dressed in a smartly tailored tuxedo, a bow tie artfully at his neck. He was an established designer of men's evening clothes in Paris. Another photo showed Albert's shop, Löw Tailleurs, at 119 Rue Lamarck. After the Nazis took control of Paris, Claire, as a French Catholic better able to move about than Józek, traveled there to urge Albert and his family to come south to Grenoble. Albert refused, believing the situation could not get worse. But, on July 16–17, 1942, the days now commemorated in France as "*La Rafle du Vel d'Hiv*," the Roundup of Jews at the Winter Stadium, Albert, his wife, and daughter were forcibly taken to the Vélodrome d'Hiver, then transported to the concentration camp at Drancy. They were later taken to Auschwitz and killed.

❦

My father wrote to Józek.

Of life in the DP camp:

"I have been elected a member of the Jewish governing committee. This is the administration of our camp. I have a bit of work...I get paid...

"In the past few weeks, we received from America several packages with food and clothes, so that our situation has improved. You don't have to worry about me, because we are managing."

Of being a DP:

"I am as healthy as a fish. I lack nothing, but one thing, stability in living. . . .

"I want finally to settle in one place and not lose more years, especially because my daughter is getting to school age and must learn some language and I wouldn't want later to interrupt her."

Of going to the United States:

"Any week now we can be called to go to America. . . .

"I was in the center of Munich several times to get information about our departure. They promise July or August, that I am first in line of the Polish persons. After all, I have been registered for a year and I've completed all the formalities."

Of concern for Józek:

"I would like to know your entire truth, everything during the period of the war, as well as in what spiritual life you are bringing up your children. As you know, I'm not old-fashioned in my views, but this is about our children's situation. I don't want to reproach you, because I think the way you act will work out best for you, and I think you know what you do."

And my father tells his surviving brother:

"I look at your photo and am glad that you found happiness in your family and can look into the eyes of the future without fear. I carry your photo at all times. I'm proud that you saved yourself and that I can say with certainty that I have a brother.

"Difficult were my years during the war, with worry about my family, those closest to me. I was waiting for the end. When I returned to familiar places I was physically and emotionally finished, because I couldn't find anyone, or traces of anyone. Days of journey followed, and, more importantly, searching for each one. At last, I received a reward for my hard struggles, for searching, turning the whole world upside down. I found you, thank God, happy with your family, and whole. I believed in you and I wasn't mistaken.

"I, also, with all my might, tried to save myself with the hope that someone would be happy that I survived, and it happened. Within this immense misfortune that befell us, we can find something to be grateful for."

21

The Red Scare

"DON'T SAY YOU WERE in Russia. They'll never let you in."
Most countries, including the United States, had quotas for immigration after the war. Many of the Jewish refugees wanted to go to the United States. Cousins Oskar, David, and Selma were processed quickly; their father in the US was already a citizen. They left by the end of 1946.

But for the rest of us the wait was long. Some DPs decided to go to Palestine—those who'd been Zionists before the war and others who now saw a Jewish state as a potential safe haven. Zionist leaders approached my father, asking him to help form the new government. But my father declined. He thought life in the new state of Israel, fighting for its existence, would be difficult. He was tired of struggling. He was concerned that my mother was becoming ill and would need medical care. So, he determined to get us into the United States.

There were many hurdles to entry: We had to have a sponsor in the US who would agree to support us financially if necessary. We had to fit within the limited quota. And, we had to pass an elaborate screening process: investigations into our history, an FBI check, a medical exam.

We were lucky. My mother found two cousins willing to sponsor us. One was Louise Springer, the daughter of Rubin, who had run away as a twelve-year old and stayed in the United States when my great grandmother Chana Shaindle took her family back to Galicia in the 1890s. Louise lived in El Paso, Texas. The other cousin was Nathan Kessler, who lived in Chicago. Louise and Nathan, who were connected as a result of our letters, decided that Chicago would be better for us: it had a large Jewish community, and jobs would be easier to get in the city. As a result, Nathan Kessler became our sponsor and Louise provided some money for our resettlement.

Finally, in 1948 our names came up in the quota system.

But, first, the screening. Between 1946, when we had started the immigration process, and 1948, the geopolitical world had changed. Countries that had been enemies during the war had become friends; former friends had become enemies.

During the war, when the Soviet Union and the United States became allies in their common struggle against Nazi Germany, the US government temporarily put aside its antipathy toward Communism and the Soviet Union. In the postwar era, however, the Soviets and the US and its western allies were at odds over ideology and Soviet control of Eastern Europe.

The relationship deteriorated so quickly that in March of 1946, Winston Churchill, the prime minister of England, declared that an "iron curtain" had descended over Europe—coining a phrase that was used throughout the Cold War. In the United States, the House Un-American Activities Committee, or HUAC, began intense efforts to find and root out "subversive Communist elements" in American society. While my family and I were still in the DP camp in 1947, HUAC began its now-infamous investigations. One involved the film industry. Actors, directors, and writers were brought before the Committee for questioning, asked to provide names of those who might be "sympathetic" to Communism. Once a person was questioned, or named, he or she became blacklisted and could no longer find work, shunned by colleagues who feared being tainted by any connection to that person.

Consequently, in Europe, among those refugees seeking to enter the United States, the fear of being labeled a Communist was pervasive. We were told that anyone who had been in the Soviet Union, for whatever reason, was suspect. Before we would be allowed to come into the United States, we would have to face interrogation to prove we were not Communists.

"Don't say you were in Russia. They'll never let you in," everyone agreed.

My parents and uncles were in a bind. They had been forced to flee their homes, were incarcerated in labor camps, were forcibly taken to Siberia. They escaped Siberia; they escaped the Soviet Union; they could have lost their lives many times over. Now there was a possibility that they would not be allowed into the United States.

They could not take the chance. Once again, in nightly sessions, they planned and plotted. They didn't think about long-term effects. They had become accustomed to doing whatever was necessary to survive.

My family reframed their history; removed all references to the Soviet Union, Siberia, Kazakhstan, Dzhambul. They kept the parts about fleeing, being caught by the Nazis, escaping. They developed a new story: that we had spent most of the war hiding in the woods, running for our lives.

How to account for my birth? Earlier, when being processed as displaced persons in Vienna, they had already changed the place of my birth, fearful of telling officials that I was born in the Soviet Union. Now they expanded the story. They coached themselves and drilled each other. They would say they couldn't remember the exact location of my birth, where they were hiding when I was born; only that it was somewhere in the vicinity of my mother's hometown, Jasło, Poland—and they made that affidavit in front of a notary stating that they were married in Jasło on September 1, 1940, proof, they thought, that they had not been in the Soviet Union.

They imagined questions the interrogators might ask and they practiced their answers: "How could you hide with a small infant?"

"We left her with a kindly Polish peasant woman from the time she was nine months old until she was two years old." During that time, they would say, they were hiding and fleeing, were incarcerated in a labor camp from which they escaped, and made their way back to get me. As the story went, I didn't recognize them and didn't want to go with them until they re-won my affections. They couldn't remember the name of the Polish woman who took care of me.

For many nights, my family sat around the table in our small room in the DP camp in Fürth, rehearsing this story. They coached me on what to say.

When interviews with the US immigration authorities in Munich were finally over, we received the necessary travel and immigration papers. All of the documentation gave my place of birth as Jasło, Poland.

But years later, comfortable in America, after surviving, after the war, my parents still felt they had to keep secrets.

Here at our sea-washed, sunset gates shall stand
A mighty woman with a torch, whose flame
Is the imprisoned lightning, and her name
Mother of Exiles. From her beacon-hand
Glows world-wide welcome; her mild eyes command
The air-bridged harbor that twin cities frame.
"Keep ancient lands, your storied pomp!" cries she
With silent lips.
"Give me your tired, your poor,
Your huddled masses yearning to breathe free,
The wretched refuse of your teeming shore.
Send these, the homeless, tempest-tost to me,
I lift my lamp beside the golden door!"

From "The New Colossus" by
Emma Lazarus; the last two
paragraphs are engraved on a
bronze plaque at the pedestal of
the Statue of Liberty.

22

Marine Tiger

ONCE WE PASSED THE interrogation by the US immigration authorities, answering their questions about how we had survived the war, we received word that we were cleared. A few months later, we were transported, in trains and trucks, to Bremen in northern Germany.

Henek and Erna in Bremen, Germany, March 1948.

Like the other European cities, Bremen was old and worn. A large statue, a man in medieval dress, still stood amidst the rubble in the center of town. It was the statue of Knight Roland, the city's symbol of civic freedom and independence. We posed at the statue's foot while Erna held up her camera and took photographs. In one photo, my father, hatless, turns his face up toward the gray and cloudy sky.

On March 7, 1948, my father wrote to Józek:

"Now the next stage is coming and it's the last one.... We are staying in a very well-organized transit point. There are a lot of apartment buildings, clean, white, good food. We are all feeling good after a trying journey from Munich with a transport which took two days and two nights. We were getting supplies of food on the way.

"So you see, dear Józek, a new phase of my life is beginning. I have good hopes... Now this year, for both of us, will start a new, happy and normal life."

US immigration gave us medical exams. Smallpox vaccinations on my upper arm left round, indented scars. We passed the medical exams.

Rather, my mother, father, me, Henek, and Erna passed. But not Tulek. He had been a sickly young boy, with every childhood illness, and appendicitis and pneumonia. He had been so ill with pneumonia, *zapalenie płuc*, that, to treat him, doctors performed surgery to remove a rib, leaving Tulek with a large, concave scar in the left middle of his back. At the medical exam before being cleared to go to the US, doctors saw Tulek's back. They wanted to conduct more tests to make certain he was healthy.

Tulek was held back. My anxious mother did not want to board the ship that would take us away from Europe and away from Tulek, but my father worked hard to convince her that her brother would follow on the next boat. Tulek did come, one month later. But my mother couldn't stop worrying, on the ship and even after he arrived.

We sailed on March 12, 1948. The ship was the SS *Marine Tiger*; we pronounced it the Polish way, "mareeneh teeger." It was a US troopship, a large vessel for its time, 523 feet long, weighing more than 12,000 tons, with a passenger capacity of 3,500.

My father to Józek: "It was a big nice looking ship…We departed at 6 p.m. By night we were on the North Sea and the second day we crossed the English Channel. On the third day we were on the Atlantic Ocean. Then the real passage began. Seasickness started, although the weather was very nice. The ship started to rock and that caused the sickness. My wife was sick all the time, myself two days. It's a very troublesome sickness, but not dangerous. The head roars, the food comes up, and at the end you can't eat anything. But it only lasts as long as you stay on the ship."

The ship was dark metal, with steep, narrow stairways leading up to different levels where American crewmen worked, always smiling and stopping to teach me a new word as I passed. Other, darker staircases led to barracks below, confined spaces where I didn't linger.

Men and women, more than a thousand of us, were placed in separate barracks. With my mother and Erna, I was in the women's barracks, a large, low-ceilinged room with cots laid out side by side. My mother was seasick and stayed on her cot for the entire voyage, getting up each morning only to brush and braid my hair.

During this voyage my relationship with my mother changed. Now I was responsible for taking care of her. I was six years old.

I'd meet my father and Henek in the dining room for meals, where we served ourselves from platters on one long table and sat at other long tables to eat. My father would prepare a plate of food for my mother, and, after I finished eating, I would take it to her as she lay on her cot in the women's barracks below deck. I'd wait a while, but I never saw her touch the food.

For the first time, I was on my own. Life in the DP camp had been a kind of cocoon, where everyone knew me and watched over me. But on the ship, I was unfettered by adult overseers. I loved the freedom to go and come wherever and whenever I wanted. In my navy

Onboard the ship.

With Henek on the ship.

snowsuit that my mother had made from an old military uniform, with a white ribbon in my hair, I explored the ship from bow to stern, scampering up staircases and across decks. Sometimes I'd run into Erna and she would photograph me looking out at the rolling gray waves, my hair and ribbon blowing in the wind, against the stark black lines of the ship.

For the adults, too, the ship held a new experience. Each person had a safe place and a clean bed. Food—as much as one could eat—was provided three times a day. No sight of land, in the middle of nowhere, the ship was seemingly not connected to the survivors' lives of pain. They could stand on deck, breathe salty air, feel cool breezes and look to an unlimited horizon.

The voyage lasted eleven days.

On the last morning, after an early breakfast, I went out on deck with my father, Henek, and Erna. We stood at the rail. Many of the passengers were also on deck, searching for the New York harbor. My father lifted me up on Henek's shoulders. Then he went below, into the women's barracks, and came back with my mother, gently propelling her by the small of her back. She was wearing a dark wool coat,

On the ship to America.

way too big for her. My father eased her to the front of the railing and pointed to a dark speck in the distance. She stared wordlessly, dark hollows around her eyes. My father reached up to me, where I still sat on Henek's shoulders, and put me down, placing me in front of him. I held on to the rail.

"*Uważaj*," my father said. "Look there."

Everybody seemed to be talking at once. "The Statue of Liberty. She's greeting us to America." Against the overcast gray sky, I saw a tiny dark speck in the distance. Gradually it became bigger and took on the form of the statue of the goddess with one arm in the air. Next to me, Erna held her Leica to her eye. *Whirr, snap*, I heard as she took a photo, then *whirr, snap*, again and again.

My father was very still, one hand on my mother's elbow.

All of us stood as the ship passed close to the Statue of Liberty, still framed by an overcast sky. Then shore approached.

My father described it in another letter to Józek: "We arrived on the 23rd of March at 3 a.m., and we were waiting until 8 to enter the port. We saw beautiful views in the morning from the ship, the Statue of Liberty, and a huge city. After the formalities we disembarked on land at noon. In the port, relatives from New York waited for us."

They wore warm coats, those relatives, who smiled and smelled of bread.

Adieu mon cœur.
On te jette au malheur.
Tu n'auras pas mes yeux
Pour mourir . . .
Adieu mon cœur.
Les échos du bonheur
Font tes chants tristes
Autant qu'un repentir.

Good-bye my heart.
It is plunged into sadness
You will not have my eyes
For death . . .
Good-bye my heart.
The sounds of good cheer
At the bottom of sad songs
Will be as a repentance.

From "Adieu Mon Coeur,"
words by Henri Contet, music
by Marguerite Monnot
Sung by Edith Piaf, 1946

23

The Golden Land

I N NEW YORK WHERE we disembarked, I stared at a landscape of gray sidewalks and tall gray buildings, and wondered at the lack of green trees and brown earth. Where were the streets of gold? Many people, adults and older children, well dressed, round and cheery, spoke to us in Yiddish and took photographs.

We visited each relative's home. The New York cousins gave me a fine hand-me-down pink dress trimmed in lace, brown knee socks, and a brown sweater. They gave us food—a plate of strawberries and sour cream topped with sugar. I'd never tasted sour cream; it was rich and thick. But sugar on top was too much, too sweet.

"*Rózia, ja dobrze zrobiłem w Ameryce, nie?*" my mother's cousin Monek asked with pride, spreading his arms wide, standing in the center of the living room of his three-room apartment in Queens, New York. He asked if we agreed how well he did in America. He strutted among his floral print couch, his maroon chair, several small tables, and a large assortment of knickknacks. Everything was spotless and carefully positioned in the small room.

"*Tak. Na pewno.*" Yes, of course, my mother responded. We looked in awe at all the Pretty Things of the Life of Plenty.

"Monek used to play the violin," my mother told us. "He made it sing. He performed in small concerts, in restaurants. Everyone hoped he would become famous.

"Monek's mother thought no girl was good enough for him. But he fell in love with Escza. Escza's family was rich. Then, in 1929, Escza's family left for the United States. The next year, Monek followed her. His mother was heartbroken. On the day he left, we all went to the train station to see him off. As the train pulled out of the station, Monek's mother ran after the train, running down the tracks, sobbing. Everyone in town talked about it for years after."

That first day in America, I met Monek's wife, Escza. Everything about her was round. Her eyebrows were painted in a half-moon on her round face, her lips in a bee-sting shape. Her hair was frizzy and unnaturally dark, and she had a "thick" tongue. Her speech was hard to understand. She wore a gray suit and high heels. Her perfume was so sweet, so strong.

I sat next to her on a small folding chair; she was seated on a maroon easy chair. I admired the shoulder of her suit, reached out. "I don't like to be touched," she told me sharply.

I drew back.

When I was older, I thought about how Monek left his family, his country, his career, and his future to follow her—and she didn't like to be touched. In the United States, Monek became a waiter and only played the violin once in a while, in an amateur orchestra.

On that first day in the United States, my father searched for his own relatives in the New York phone book, his mother's sister and two brothers who had immigrated to America years earlier. He found one of the telephone numbers and called; a man's voice, my father's uncle C, answered.

"*Ich hob gekumen,*" my father said in Yiddish, after identifying himself. "I've arrived from Europe, from a DP camp in Germany."

"Well, what do you want?" C replied. "We have no money for you."

My father hung up the phone. He never again spoke to C. Years later he told me how deeply hurt he was by C's response. He vowed, then and there, never to ask anyone for help. He would depend only on himself.

❧

My parents and I spent our night in New York in one cousin's small apartment; Erna and Henek were in another. The next day, cousins took us to the train station. During the nineteen-hour train ride from New York to Chicago, we each had a place to sit the entire way; luxury already.

At Union Station in Chicago, Oskar's older brother, David, met us. He was dressed in a fine navy blue overcoat with big buttons; he looked older and his hair was smooth. He and others took us to the home of Nathan Kessler, our sponsor.

On March 27, 1948, my father wrote again to Józek:

"We traveled to Chicago to other relatives who had helped us when we were in Germany. They brought us from the train station in their cars. All the relatives came to their apartment, welcomes and storytelling into the night. At once they started debating about our future. For now they are looking for a place to live for us. We are all feeling well, healthy, but now we'll also have to get adjusted to things."

For the first month, my mother, father, and I lived in a rented room. Then my uncle Tulek arrived, having finally been permitted to immigrate, and the four of us moved into our own apartment on Chicago's southwest side. Erna and Henek had their own apartment. The men found work.

May 2, 1948, my father to Józek:

"You're no doubt curious about how I live here. I live with my wife, child, and one brother-in-law. I go to work; the work consists of standing in a store with women's fabrics and I'm learning everything from scratch, that is language and knowing the goods, selling, packaging and so on.

"I earn 34 dollars per week. That is the beginning for me. I hope it will be better later. But here is the rule, don't worry, take everything lightly. Maybe I could do that...

"Let's be realistic, the time will come, one has to be patient…
"When I'm able, I'll stop being 'green.'"

☙

For me, Chicago was brick homes, cousins, tables laden with food, especially chicken soup, wonderful hand-me-down clothes, comfortable hand-me-down furniture. I loved the variety and abundance of food and grew chubby. Fanny, Nathan Kessler's wife, gave me a doll. I started school.

And my mother—well, my mother began her attempt to live a "normal life."

Ja, nie wiadomo czemu,
Obńořony ksiźgami
Proroków i teologów,
Filozofów, poetów,
Szukańem odpowiedzi
Marszcząc siź, wykrzywiając, budząc siź w środku nocy
Wykrzykując nad ranem.
Niestety moja pamiźź
Nie chciańa mnie opuściź,
A w niej ŕywe istoty
Kańda z jej wńasnym bólem,
Kańda z jej wńasną śmiercią,
Z jej wńasnym przeraŕeniem.
Do kogo mam siź zwróciż
z tą cańkiem ciemną sprawą
Bólu i razem winy
W architekturze świata,
Jeŕeli tutaj nisko
Ni tam w górze wysoko
ŕadna moc nie obali
Przyczyny i skutku?

I, for unknown reasons,
Surrounded by the books
Of prophets and theologians,
Of philosophers, poets,
Searched for an answer,
Scowling, grimacing,
Waking up at night, muttering at dawn.
Alas, my memory
Does not want to leave me
And in it, live beings
Each with its own pain,

Each with its own dying,
Its own trepidation.
To whom should I turn
With that affair so dark
Of pain and also guilt
In the structure of the world,
If either here below
Or over there on high
No power can abolish
The cause and the effect?

From "Wiersz na koniec
stulecia" ("Poem for the End
of the Century") by Czesław
Miłosz

24

My Mother, Rózia—1948

ONE NIGHT, MY MOTHER disappeared.

"You shouldn't have let them take her!" Tulek shouted.

My father remained silent, jaw clenched. I left for my new school.

My father was home when I returned. We hardly talked, eating a silent supper of *grishik*, cream of wheat, with milk. He gave me a soft hug and tucked me in for the night, but later, when I got up to go to the bathroom, he was staring into the bathroom mirror, muttering, "You don't know what you're talking about." I knew he was answering Tulek. But I knew nothing more.

After that, my father and I lived alone in our long apartment, the faded green couch in the front room, the cavernous dining room, the long hallway, the dark kitchen opening onto the quiet back porch. My father slept in the front bedroom; my cot was in the dining room. Before, when my mother was still home, in the mornings, I'd run down the hall and jump onto Tulek's bed. The wooden boards holding the mattress would slip from the weight of my jumping, sending the mattress, Tulek, and me to the floor in a jumble. He'd wake, shout, and laugh, then tickle me till I begged him to stop. But now that my mother was gone, I didn't run down the hall, our apartment was quiet, and Tulek was not around much. He married a few months later and I was alone with my now very quiet father. I moved into the bedroom that used to be Tulek's. There, at the back of our apartment, I felt no protection between me and our dark backyard where, I imagined, all kinds of scary creatures lurked.

One afternoon, Erna took me to a movie, the first one I'd ever seen. That night, I slept in in my room at the back of the apartment. Outside the window, straddling the high branches of the tree that abutted the window, was the monstrous gorilla from the movie. Mighty Joe Young's face stared in at me with mouth wide open in a leering grin, showing his long teeth. His bloodshot eyes didn't blink, and, with each breath from his wide nostrils, more steam settled on the window. The palm of one big hairy paw settled on the window facing me. I heard scratch, scratch, then, thump, thump, as the beast raised his other fist to smash the glass. Then I heard a loud crack; my room lit up as bright as day. The hairs on my neck prickled. In the heavy humid air a fly buzzed in my ear. Another bolt of lightning lit up the room and the close sharp crack of thunder reverberated through the walls; my whole body shook with it. Opening one eye, I braved a look at the window. A large jagged sycamore leaf was plastered against the glass as several more leaves waved behind it, and the branches of the tree thumped and scratched against the outside wall. The pounding of the rain echoed the beating of my heart. I lay in my bed, alone, my sheets rumpled and stained with sweat.

At that age, I had recurrent nightmares. In one, I lived in a displaced persons camp in which the housing consisted of a labyrinth of identical tents made out of moldy gray army blankets strung up on heavy ropes. A woman Nazi, a witch, really, with a long, pointed chin and an even longer and pointier nose, abducted me and forced me, amid driving rain, through the maze of tents to a far-off musty-smelling tent, to torture me. The howling wind whipped the tent and my body back and forth. I tried to scream but no sound came out. Terrified, I woke with a start, still trying to scream, but no sound was possible out of my dry mouth. No one heard me. My mother had been taken to a place I wasn't allowed to ask about. My father was at the far end of the apartment, too far to hear. Both my uncles had married and left me. I was alone in my bed with my scratchy, damp, gray wool blanket, as outside the wind whipped the rain, slapping it violently against my window in loud, irregular torrents.

Now, I study a photograph of my mother from an earlier time, before the war, around the time of her engagement to my father. She's fashionably dressed in a dark sweater, a white collar peeking out, looking straight at the camera with dark eyes, their intensity and energy burning through the picture. She has a small scar over her lip. She told me that when she was three years old, she fell while running with a glass of water. Oh, what consternation it caused the family, this bloodied little girl, always getting into scrapes. In adulthood, the scar made her mouth look a bit insolent, adding to her mystery and allure, I always thought. But maybe her childhood fall was when it began—her many fears that made her terrified that something was wrong with me, or if it wasn't it would be. "Don't ever run with a glass in your hand," she constantly admonished, although I was never as boisterous or adventuresome as I imagine she was.

I turn from the photo of my mother before the war to a photo taken right after the war, in 1946 in the DP camp. Rózia's face is thin, her hair flat, tucked behind too-large ears. Her cheekbones are hollow, her mouth a thin line. But her eyes. Hollow orbs.

We were in the US only a few months when an acquaintance of the family asked me: "Who do you like better? Your mother or your father?"

"I like them both the same," I replied, a six-year-old who knew what was expected.

The man nodded and I was happy I gave the right answer. But, where my father was gentle and patient, smiling when he spoke in his soft voice, teasing or coaxing me, teaching me, my mother's voice was harsh and shrill: "Be careful. Why do you want to go on the swing? What if you fall? Stand up straight? Oh, why is she bent over? You'll be a hunchback. Don't get cold. Here, put on another sweater."

She held me too tight. Her hands shook. She yelled all the time.

She startled at every noise. She couldn't sit still. She got ideas and had to move furniture right away. Then move it back, every muscle straining. At night, whenever I woke up, she was always awake. I didn't see her smile or laugh.

At gatherings, my mother might speak with another woman, her cheeks flushed. Coming closer, I'd overhear, "We were in Siber..." She'd stop and shake her head. "No, we were in hiding. I don't know. Don't ask me." Then, silence. Unable to tell the truth, my mother couldn't keep the story straight. At home, my father told me not to ask her questions, not to talk about the past.

"*Nerwowa*," my father said. "She's nervous."

After my mother disappeared, no one told me why. Over time, I understood she was sick. I thought worry about me had made my mother sick. For as long as I could remember, my mother had been obsessed with my well-being, concerned that I would become somehow imperfect or physically deformed because of the deprivations of my childhood. In the DP camp in Fürth, when I was five, it was my posture.

"We must find a doctor," she yelled at my father.

"She's fine," my father replied, patiently.

"A specialist," my mother insisted, "the best." Her voice rose. "She must be straight."

My father gave in. We traveled by train to a special doctor in Nuremberg, who engineered a metal frame as a back brace. The first day I wore it, I felt uncomfortable and unhappy as the bulky contraption under my light blue dress forced my body into a stiff and awkward posture. I could hardly walk; I could only stand at attention like a soldier. While my friends ran and jumped, I perched on the edge of a swing, watching.

That night, my father took charge. "This is foolishness!" he proclaimed, removing the brace and throwing it away. I sighed with relief and gratitude as my body returned to its normal curves. My father is kind, my mother is mean is how it settled in my childish mind. But I have been plagued with scoliosis all my life.

During our first summer in the United States, in an effort to help us adjust to the new country, a well-meaning social service agency sent my mother and me to a summer retreat for mothers and children in the countryside, about thirty miles from Chicago. For three weeks, I played with other children, swimming, hiking, playing ball, and learning American ways: watching and imitating, listening and mimicking. I stayed away from my mother as much as I could, avoiding her anxious looks. That was not difficult because mothers bunked in one area, children in another.

The retreat was not therapeutic for my mother. When we returned home, my mother's fears and anxieties seemed to have increased. My father was unable to soothe her agitation or answer her shouts. He could not make her eat. Then, one day, she disappeared.

❦

My mother was institutionalized for more than two years. After the first year, she came home for a few days at a time, and then for longer periods. My father seldom took me to visit her, telling me it was too painful for her. When I saw her, I had to look "perfect." Once, I had a small cut on my index finger. I wanted attention, for someone to notice that I was hurt, so I ostentatiously put a large Band-Aid on the cut. But when my father saw it, he said, "Better take that off. It will upset your mother."

I never knew the cause of my mother's illness. I have only these memories of unconnected events, none of them providing a clue. Even when I became an adult, it was never clear to me what had happened, what her behavior had been like, why her treatment was necessary. My father and uncles refused to speak about it. All my mother acknowledged, many years later, was: "I had a breakdown."

As I grew, I read everything I could about mental illness. At fifteen, I read Sigmund Freud. Maybe I would become a psychiatrist and get to the bottom of my mother's illness. Maybe I could make her whole. But I found no answers in *The Interpretation of Dreams*, or in Freud's lengthy psychoanalytic approaches.

Why did my mother break while my father and others, though hurt and sad, were able to continue? Was it an inherited weakness? Would I become ill too? I worried that there was some darkness in me that would be revealed when I turned thirty-four, the age my mother was when she disappeared.

When my mother became ill, nothing had been written about post-traumatic stress disorder. Treatment of depression was still in its "snake pit" stage. Survivor's guilt was a new term. There were no studies of hormonal imbalances, only theories of female "hysteria." And there were no medical studies that suggested malnutrition or vitamin deficiencies could affect a person's mental state.

Early in my mother's hospitalization, a Dr. Steinfeld, a respected psychiatrist trained in Germany, said my mother's condition was incurable. In despair, my father gave his consent to the treatment Dr. Steinfeld recommended—electric shock therapy. Such therapy was still experimental; in those years massive doses were used. My mother—tomboy, spunky girl, love-struck young woman, capable career person, loyal sister, doting mother, survivor of beatings by a Nazi soldier, forced labor in Siberia, harsh life in Kazakhstan, homeless wanderings, starvation and deprivation—my mother was given electric shock treatments, first once a week, then once a month, for two years. Each time, she was strapped to a table, a bar between her teeth, while electric currents coursed through her system, her body convulsing, her mouth foaming, and her eyeballs rolling back in her head. This was done under the supervision of Dr. Steinfeld in the Des Plaines Sanitarium, outside of Chicago, Illinois, USA, in 1948, 1949, and 1950.

❦

When I was nine, my mother came home to stay. My father brought her inside during my birthday party. My friends and I were sitting in the kitchen eating birthday cake. I saw a body shuffle through the front door and slip into the front bedroom. The body was gaunt, its shoulders bony; it could barely stand. It was my mother who stared at me with expressionless eyes. Who didn't speak. Who didn't smile. Who couldn't dress herself. Who didn't remember how to cook.

Now, everything was in slow motion. I escaped to school and my friends.

Demain il fera jour.
C'est quand tout est perdu
Que tout commence.
Demain il fera jour.
Après l'amour,
Un autre amour commence.
Un petit gars viendra en sifflotant,
Demain . . .
Il aura les bras chargés de printemps,
Demain . . .
Les cloches sonneront dans votre ciel,
Demain . . .
Tu verras la lune de miel briller,
Demain . . .
Car demain :
Tu vas sourire encore,
Aimer encore, souffrir encore,
Toujours . . .
Demain il fera jour.

Tomorrow it will be day.
When all is lost
All begins.
Tomorrow it will be day.
After love,
Another love begins.
A small wind will float
Tomorrow...
There will be arms filled with spring
Tomorrow...
The bells will ring in the sky
Tomorrow....
You will see the bright honey moon
Tomorrow...
Because tomorrow:
You will laugh again,
Love again, suffer again,
Always...
Tomorrow it will be day.

"Demain (il fera jour)"
Words by Marcel Achard,
music by Marguerite Monnot,
sung by Edith Piaf, 1951

25

School

"WHEN YOU SPEAK ENGLISH, you have to talk like you have hot potatoes in your mouth," Erna told me on the ship coming to the United States.

Speaking English was harder than speaking other languages. English pronunciation was a problem for those of us who were used to the round sounds of Polish. Spoken English sounded "slushy," slurred. We didn't speak English at home, so I had to pay careful attention to the sounds when I was in school.

I started first grade as soon as we arrived in Chicago. My teacher, Miss Weinstein, had a wide lipstick-rimmed smile. "Don't worry, she knows Yiddish," the principal reassured my parents before they left me there on my first day. But Miss Weinstein wasn't comfortable with Yiddish and I struggled through the days, intuiting from gesture and expression.

Reading English was also difficult. In Polish, every letter or combination of letters has a distinct pronunciation; there are no silent letters. In English, there are many silent letters, and the rules are not consistent. I was constantly confused. Miss Weinstein wrote the word "w-h-a-t" on the blackboard and called on a classmate to read it. "Wot," the classmate pronounced. Oh, I realized, the *h* must be silent. Then, Miss Weinstein wrote "w-h-o" on the blackboard and called on me. Using my newfound logic, "wo," I read, loud and clear. The class exploded in laughter. My face felt hot.

But I learned fast, and by the following year, my second grade teacher recommended that I be double promoted, "skipped" one half year to the third grade.

Language was not the only difficult thing to learn in this new country. I also had to learn the customs. But I was alone: my mother was "away," my father worked, and my uncles had their own busy lives. So I figured things out on my own. For my seventh birthday, I gave myself a party. I got a dollar from my father and walked to the store down the street to buy invitations and decorations. I delivered the invitations to my friends in the neighborhood. I got some more money and bought a cake. When everything was ready, one hour before the party, I knew it was time for action. I put on my new green coat; it was double-breasted with two rows of buttons down the front, a green belt, and a fake fur collar. I attached a big tag to one of the buttons that proclaimed: "I am 7 years old." Then I proudly pro-ceeded to walk around the neighborhood, ringing doorbells to pick up my guests for my party.

At the fourth or fifth stop, one mother told me, "It's not right to pick up your guests. You should stay home and wait for everyone to come to you."

Surprised and hurt, I asked: "But what if everyone forgets and no one comes?"

"You just wait," was the answer. By that time, my friends were already gathered, so we came to my home, and I remember the party as a great success. And although I still worry that guests won't show up at a party, I never drive around to pick them up.

During those years when my mother was "away," my father worked long hours, even on weekends. The Hebrew Immigrant Aid Society, HIAS, sent a succession of housekeepers to clean and prepare meals. In the mornings, before the housekeeper arrived, I took care of myself. I didn't know people brushed their teeth; I'd never seen the adults I lived with brushing their teeth. So that was not one of my rituals. I couldn't yet brush my own hair. I was chubby. My clothes were often ill-fitting hand-me-downs.

One morning I stopped to pick up an even younger girl who I walked to school as a favor to her mother. Her mother looked at me and rearranged my clothes, tugging at my shorts to put them right. She was kind, but her attention almost made me cry.

Another time, I wore what I thought was a new outfit I had received as a gift: yellow seersucker shorts and a sleeveless shirt with brown rickrack trim. Another kindly mother down the street pointed out, to my humiliation, that I was wearing pajamas.

Once a week, my father washed and combed my long hair. I loved that ritual. I loved the two nights a week that my father came home from work early. I loved those nights when, after dinner, he and I would sit at the dining room table, my father watching and helping me with my homework. It seemed to me that there was not anything my father didn't know.

Most of the time, though, I was alone. After school, I'd let myself into our apartment. The front rooms were dark, but there was always a light in the kitchen where the housekeeper of the day sat drinking her tea. Melodramatic voices came from the radio as Stella Dallas tried to save her home from the unscrupulous lender, or herself from the sweatshop, or her child from something or other. The housekeepers' names and faces varied; one was nice; one yelled at my friends, and my father called HIAS and they sent another; but they all seemed to listen to Stella Dallas. And very few had time to talk to me.

During our first few years in Chicago, we lived in the upstairs apartment of a two-family brick house on the city's southwest side. Our apartment had six rooms. You'd go up the stairs and enter the apartment in its middle into the dining room. A rectangular table and six chairs stood in the center of the room, and my cot sat against a side wall. The living room, or front room, was to the left of the dining room and faced the street. It was furnished with a pine-framed green sofa and chair, hand-me-down furniture sent by the cousins in Texas.

A door from the living room led to the front bedroom, used by my parents. The back half of the apartment held the kitchen, bathroom and back bedroom. Another dark room off the dining room was used for storage.

The house was owned by the Abramsons, who lived in the apartment downstairs: Mr. and Mrs. Abramson, their three sons in their twenties, and a daughter, Irene, seventeen. Irene was slim and graceful with long legs, defined, neat hips, and a slim waist. Beside her, I was an awkward eight-year-old. She wore tight jeans; I wore a voluminous plaid skirt.

On warm summer nights, the two of us sat on the front porch or on the stairs to the sidewalk, watching "the action." At six o'clock each night, mothers called their children to dinner. "Yoooosel!" a large Yiddish mother in a faded shapeless cotton dress yodeled from her front porch. At the other end of the block, an equally large black grandmother in a colorful print robe would shriek "Guv-nuh," her voice rising on the second syllable.

On some nights, my uncle Tulek, called Nathan now by Americans, played cards with the Abramson boys. They'd sit around the table in the Abramson dining room late into the night, smoking and playing poker. I'd sit with them, following the game with Tulek. "'Nusha," he'd ask me, "What should I play next?"

"New Shoe," the Abramson boys would tease, a wordplay on my nickname. I studied the cards, toyed with the chips, and finally fell asleep with my head on the table. My father came and carried me upstairs.

Then Tulek got married.

※

Tulek had wanted to marry an American girl. But now that he was finally in the United States, who should he happen to meet? Two sisters he had flirted with in the DP camp in Fürth at the Purim costume party—the Pogorelsky sisters. Everyone thought Tulek would pair with the younger sister, Doba, but they didn't get along, both too volatile. Tulek now gravitated to the older sister, Riva, who was pretty and soft-spoken.

Tulek and Riva were married in January, 1949. I was seven. I was the flower girl. Tulek bought me the prettiest dress I had ever seen, floor-length blue satin with ruffles around the neck.

On the morning of the wedding, a Sunday, I went downstairs and asked Irene to help me fix my hair. I knew just how I wanted to look. I showed Irene a picture I found of a dreamy-eyed girl in a ruffled dress, her hair a cascade of ringlets. Irene washed my hair, then carefully sectioned my long hair, rolling each strand flat against my head and securing it with a bobby pin. She told me to leave my hair like that to dry until later that day.

At about four o'clock, I went downstairs again.

"I'm going out on a date now," Irene said, rushing to the door. "Finish your hair yourself. You can do it."

So I got ready for the wedding myself. I carefully removed the bobby pins from my head and, not knowing what else to do, I left the tightly coiled strands flat on my head. A photograph taken at Tulek's wedding shows me in my ruffled dress, a small smile displaying a missing front tooth, and my hair tightly packed in round flat circles around my head. No cascade of ringlets. Irene had not told me the coiled strands were supposed to be brushed out.

It was the first wedding I ever attended. I was excited and happy for the attention I got walking down the aisle as the flower girl. But, later, an old man—they all seemed old to me—asked, "Why are you dressed like that?"

"I'm the flower girl."

"No, you're not," he said, teasingly.

"Yes, I am." I stamped my foot as hot tears spilled down my cheeks. I didn't like this American. I wanted my mother. She would tell him, yes. I was the flower girl.

Flower girl at Tulek's wedding.

Ucz się dziecino, bo lata płyną,
Dzien po roku przepada w zmroku.
Ci co pracują przyszłość budują,
Oni nie zginą ucz się dziecino.

Study, young girl, for the years swim past,
Day after year falls into shadow.
Those who work build the future,
They will not be lost. Study, young girl.

Polish poem

26

✄

Becoming an American Girl

SUPERMAN, ARCHIE AND VERONICA, Nancy and Sluggo, Batman and Robin. I read them all. Devoured them. Whenever my father gave me a dime, I ran to the newsstand two blocks away and bought more comic books. I had three, four hundred. After my mother came home, she sold them back to the newsstand owner for five cents each. Sometimes I bought the same ones again, not remembering I had already read them.

On weekends, my friends Nolan and Sharon gathered at my house to read the comic books, sprawling on the couch or floor of the living room.

Weekdays, I'd come home from school, prepare a snack of bologna on white bread, balance the sandwich on one arm of the easy chair and a plateful of grapes on the other arm, and sit down with my stack of comics.

That's how I learned real English. At school I was taught to speak and write formally. But in comic books, I learned casual expressions and slang. Americans have a different culture from the British or other English-speaking countries. Americans used expressions like "gee whiz," "wow," "shabam!" Americans know about kryptonite, the Bat Cave, Wonder Woman. To really be American, one has to read comic books.

I read other books too. For a while, I was obsessed with biographies of Abraham Lincoln, the boy who was born in a log cabin and became president of the United States. But comic books were the real thing to me. "Has anyone read *A Tale of Two Cities?*" my fourth grade teacher asked. I raised my hand confidently, the only one in the class to do so. The teacher was impressed. Much later, I realized the teacher was asking about the book by Charles Dickens, not the Classics Illustrated comic book. I didn't read the real book until six years later.

Television also taught me American ways. During our first year in our new country, on many nights, my father and I watched television in the Abramsons' apartment. Sitting on a scratchy gray sofa, we focused on the black-and-white thirteen-inch picture in a dark wooden box at the other end of the room. On election eve, 1948, we watched the presidential returns come in, neck-and-neck for Dewey and Truman. I didn't understand what was happening, but everyone seemed excited and talked all at once as they watched and listened.

After school, my friends and I would gather at my friend Nolan's house to watch *Howdy Doody.* "It's Howdy Doody time," Buffalo Bob sang as the grinning puppet bounced and Clarabell the clown honked his horn. Other times, we might watch *Hopalong Cassidy* or *The Lone Ranger.* Then we'd chase each other around the sidewalks of our neighborhood, playing cowboys with "six-shooters," toy guns, strapped on belts around our waists. We'd put a strip of powdered paper, called caps, into our guns, and when we pulled the trigger the gun made a loud crack and set off smoke.

The Abramsons had a black telephone on a stand in their front hallway. If my father and I needed to make a telephone call, we'd go downstairs and ask permission to use their phone. In those days, you'd pick up the phone and ask the operator for a number. The phone was not private; it was a party line, and sometimes the other party was talking when you picked up the phone. Protocol required that you hang up and try again later; you weren't supposed to listen to the other party's call. When your phone rang, you had to count the rings for your code: one ring might mean the call was for you, two rings for the other party sharing the line.

We paid the Abramsons rent of fifty dollars a month. My father earned thirty-five dollars a week. But we were not yet into having things, so we were thrifty. Despite the fact that we were immigrants and the Abramsons owned the building, we always seemed to have more ready money. Sometimes the Abramson boys, or Irene, would come up to our apartment and ask for an advance on the rent. My father kept a log they signed each time he gave them an advance. By the end of the month, we might not owe them anything at all.

In 1949, my father bought us our own television, a DeForest. Now we watched at home, a different special program every night. One day, I couldn't wait to tell my father about a great show I had heard about that we had to watch. "It's called *I Love Lucy*," I informed him almost as soon as he walked in the door. "But it's not a love story," I hastened to add, concerned he might think it was mushy and not want to watch.

"Anyway," I added with all the seriousness I could muster, relaying something else I had heard that day, "television is all commercial, you know." I didn't know what the word meant, but it sounded important. My father nodded and smiled at me.

〜

For three weeks during the summer I was eight, I went to Sunset Camp in Bartlett, Illinois. It was a sleepaway camp operated by the Max Straus Center, a Chicago social service agency. The excitement started at Union Station in Chicago, where we gathered for the one-hour train ride to camp. All the girls who had been there before, the American girls, met their friends, laughing and shouting out names. By my second year of going to camp, I, too, was running through the train station looking for friends from the previous year. We'd board the train for the anticipation-filled ride to Bartlett, Illinois. Counselors would meet the train, and we'd quickly hunt for our favorite counselors to share the hike along a highway to a leafy unpaved road and, finally, around a bend to camp: the first view the dining hall, then the lake with its half-moon beach, and beyond that the five cabins. My view of heaven.

I took to every inch of that place. I loved the large dining hall with its screened porch, the upright piano where someone was always playing *Chopsticks*, the book corner, the rows of tables with benches, the songs and spirit at meal times. I even loved the camp food, which I thought abundant and imaginative: crunchy Rice Krispies and other cold cereals; hot, round, doughy corn fritters, so exotic to me; hot dogs, ever so much better than liverwurst. Oh, and campfires. S'mores. We slept in three-room bunks, six girls in one room, three counselors in the middle room, and six more girls in the room on the other side. My chubby little girl's heart fell for the counselors, those American women of nineteen or twenty, with their easy approach, good looks, and quick smiles. How I admired them and longed to be like them.

Only visiting days were not fun. Everyone's parents came. My mother was "away" and my father had to work on Sunday. As my friends met their mothers and fathers, the counselors kept me occupied. We'd sit in a field and look for four-leaf clovers, or we'd hike down the road and back, just me and a counselor, and talk about what we'd wish for if we found a four-leaf clover. I never mentioned my mother.

My father was given a special visiting day, usually a Tuesday when he didn't have to work. I would show him my bunk and proudly introduce my American counselors, Punky or Lee, Corky or Monee. Later, he sat on a bench at the lake while I ran into the water and showed off my swim strokes. I swam to the middle of the small lake, dove off the ramp, forward or backward, I was fearless, and then I swam swiftly back to shore. After that, my father and I walked to the rec field and found a shady spot where we sat on the grass. Voices and laughter came from the dining hall as I watched my father unlatch his leather satchel, spread out a napkin, and take out pungent liverwurst and rye bread sandwiches. By the afternoon he was gone and I went back to my American friends.

I learned more "American" ways at camp. I played baseball, rode horseback, went to cookouts, sang songs, heard folk tales, read Nancy Drew mysteries, and giggled with my friends at the scary stories the counselors read aloud at bedtime. The end of one chapter was a grabber: Nancy Drew "turned and saw Scarface lurking in the bushes." We repeated the words like a mantra all the next day until it was time to hear the next chapter.

Then there were camp songs; I loved the joyous group singing. "I've been working on the railroad," we'd sing. Or a round: "Row, row, row your boat, gently down the stream," with one group starting after the other had finished the first line. Gentle songs: "Down in the valley, the valley so low, hang your head over, hear the wind blow." Energetic songs: "She'll be coming round the mountain when she comes, toot, toot."

On the Fourth of July, when we put on a pageant, I proudly carried the American flag as my friend Deena read "Barbara Frietchie," the poem about the American Civil War:

"Shoot, if you must, this old grey head,
But spare your country's flag," she said.

Yes. I was an American girl.

Are you sleeping, are you sleeping,
Brother John, Brother John?
Morning bells are ringing, morning bells are ringing,
Ding ding dong, ding ding dong

French:
Frère Jacque, Frère Jacque,
Dormez-vous, dormez-vous?
Sonnez les matines, sonnez les matines,
Ding dang dong, ding dang dong.

Polish:
Panie Janie, Panie Janie
Rano wstan! Rano wstan!
Wszystkie dzwony biją, Wszystkie dzwony biją
Bim bam bum, bim bam bum.

Russian:
Bratez Jakow, Bratez Jakow,
Spish li ti, spish li ti?
Slishish zwon na bashne, slishish zwon na bashne,
Ding dang dong, ding dang dong.

German:
Bruder Jakob, Bruder Jakob,
Schläfts du noch, schläfts du noch?
Hörst du nicht die glocken, hörst du nicht die glocken,
Ding ding dong, ding ding dong.

27

The Names We Had

"How many names do you have, anyway?" my cousin Beverly asks, laughing.

I don't tell her that her name has also been a source of amusement to my American husband, Richard. Beverly's Polish name is Bosia. My mother had a habit of complaining to God, in Polish, walking around the house, "*Oy, Boże, Boże.*"

"Why is your mother calling on Beverly?" Richard would ask, with a twinkle in his eye, making fun of his own inability to distinguish Polish sounds.

Richard's name is straightforward. Sometimes his mother called him Richie, or his father called him Rich. People who don't know him occasionally call him Dick. But there are no secrets in his name.

Survivors of the Holocaust took or were given new names after coming to America. In the Old World, we had Polish names and Hebrew-Yiddish names. Now we also acquired American names.

My uncle Henek, Jeheskiel in Hebrew, became Henry, an easy transition. Henry also made a relatively quick transition to the new world. His trade as a printer was a portable and useful occupation, and his second wife, Erna, was instrumental in creating a good new life.

Tulek, whose formal and Hebrew name was Naftali, became Nathan, also a logical choice. He, too, seemed comfortable in his new identity, quickly taking up the offer of his uncle, Sam Gans, to go into the business of house painting. Within a year of coming to the United States, Nathan married and, shortly after, had two children.

My mother, Rózia, was Raizl in Yiddish. Her formal name was Rozalia. When we came to this country she became Rose. This name, too, seemed logical; Rózia means rose in Polish. But "I don't like Rose," she said over and over.

My father's Polish name was Mundek. His formal Hebrew-Yiddish name was Mojżesz Samuel. In his immigration papers he changed the spelling to Moses, but on his citizenship papers, six years later, he was Murray. He was encouraged to use this name by a cousin of my mother, who had himself taken the name Murray upon immigration. My father disliked the name, or when people called him Morris or Mo. He didn't complain about it or correct them, but his mouth would tighten—this wasn't his name. This wasn't his intended life.

And me! At birth, my Polish name was Anna. It's the Polish version of the first part of my Hebrew name, Chana, or Hannah as I now spelled it. The second part of my Hebrew name is Shaindel, from the Yiddish word for pretty. My Hebrew name holds the history of our lost family. I was named after my mother's formidable maternal grandmother, Chana Shaindel, the one who came to the United States in the 1890s but returned to Poland two years later, proverbially because she didn't like the secular life in the United States. I've never used the name Hannah Shaindel. It appears only on religious documents and my wedding ketubah.

"Anna" wasn't used much, either. My family called me affectionate diminutives like Anusia (pronounced Anusha), sometimes shortened to Nusha and Nushu. "New shoe" our American neighbors, the Abramsons, teased.

My mother and Tulek gave me other nicknames: Hanneleh, Tateleh, or Mameleh, which Tulek shortened over time to Mama or *Ma.* On greeting, Tulek would yell out, "Hi, Mama" while giving me a big bear hug. A friend once asked why my uncle called me Mama, but I couldn't easily explain. "Just his pet name for me," I said, shrugging.

Another diminutive of Anna, used only by my father, was Antzik, or, when he was being playful, Tzik Tzik, or simply Tzik. One night, at thirteen, my first time going alone to an evening movie to meet friends, I was walking home, four long, dark blocks on Chicago's northwest side. As I turned a corner, I saw a shadow and felt someone following me. I walked faster, but the footsteps behind me came faster too. My heart was beating so loudly, I could barely hear the sound behind me: "Tzik." The reassuring sound of my father.

Shortly after we arrived in America, my parents wanted a more American name for me. I never understood their choice, but they decided the name Alina was American, and that's how I started first grade. But my first grade teacher, Miss Weinstein, suggested that Alina should be spelled the American way, with two *e*s instead of an *i*: Aleena.

I disliked my made-up name. Americans misspelled and mispronounced it. Immigrants couldn't understand it. I wanted an "American" name, an easier name, just as I hoped for an easier life, a happy, frivolous life, an American life.

At eight, when I went to Sunset Camp, the train brought us campers to the train station in Bartlett, Illinois, and from there we hiked to camp. My footsteps crunched on the gravel, my toes hurt in my stiff new brown oxfords, but the counselor's question hurt most of all. "What's your name?" she asked those of us with whom she was walking. "Joan," "Francine," "Barbara," were the replies.

The counselor turned to me. "And yours?" she asked.

"Aleena," I answered quietly.

"Do you have a middle name?"

I paused. Others had a middle name. I should have a middle name. My Hebrew name is Hannah Shaindel. Aleena corresponds to Hannah, but what corresponds to Shaindel? It should start with "sh." I had a friend named Sharon. That had an American sound.

"I think my middle name is Sharon, but I've never used it."

"Okay, then, we'll call you Sherry."

I was Sherry all that summer and loved it. All the awards I received at ceremonies around the campfire went to a very American girl, who was just like all the other American girls, who could swim and play baseball and hike and toast marshmallows, and be casual, having the easy name of Sherry.

At home, I was still Aleena, still burdened with my family's heavy history and my feelings of responsibility for their happiness. I was serious, obedient, a good student; but I wanted to be casual and light, "American."

At fourteen, my best friend was Deena. Deena was American, chubby and intelligent, yearning for a more casual, popular persona.

"We should have nicknames," Deena said.

"Okay," I replied. "I'll call you Dee."

"What can we call you?" Deena thought aloud: "Deena, Dee, Aleena...I've got it! We'll call you Lee."

An American girl.

Is there no balm in Gilead?
Is there no physician there?
Why then is not the health
Of the daughter of my people recovered?

Oh that my head were water,
And mine eyes a fountain of tears,
That I might weep day and night
For the slain of the daughter of my people.

Jeremiah 8: 22 and 9:1

28

Talking About It

T HE SURVIVORS WANTED TO forget. They wanted their children to live "normal" lives, untainted by a sad history. They stopped talking about their past, even as they remained haunted by it. They thought no one would believe, could believe, where they'd been, what had happened. It was beyond imagination.

They recreated their lives: work, home, family, friends. They negotiated the streets and shops of Chicago, learned American ways, tried American foods. They shopped, cooked, made small talk with neighbors, learned to drive. They attended synagogue, got together at holidays, embraced Thanksgiving. They studied English, read newspapers, watched TV. Those who were not yet married found mates, had children, sent these children to school. The children had no accents, didn't know Polish or Yiddish, so the survivors spoke more English and learned more American ways.

In my family, Erna, who had always been the first to pick up new trends, was the quickest to learn. She didn't leave Henry after we came to the United States, as Nathan had predicted. Instead, she threw her energies into creating a "good life." Erna and Henry bought a small printing business of their own. Henry managed the print shop and Erna managed the business office.

As their business improved, Erna and Henry's living conditions changed. Their first apartment was a small basement studio. Within a year, they moved into a four-room apartment on the second floor of a two-family frame house on Chicago's north side. My father and I visited them there in December of 1948, our first year in the United States. As the adults talked around the kitchen table, I got up and wandered to the back door, opened it, and stepped out to the back porch. The air was cold and had a woodsy smell. Astonishing to me, I saw a green Christmas tree, about four feet tall, festooned with shiny red and green ornaments. My father looked through the open door, but Erna grabbed my hand, brought me inside, and closed the door quickly.

"The landlady," Erna said in Polish. "I don't want her to know we're Jewish. She wouldn't let us stay."

"*Ach, cholera*," Henry cursed softly.

My father said nothing about the tree throughout dinner, but later, going home on the streetcar, he mused, "Maybe Erna pretended to be Christian for so long she can't stop. She's still afraid to be Jewish."

The Christmas tree appeared on Erna and Henry's porch for several Christmases.

Then, in 1955, they bought a house in the suburb of Skokie. From then on, Erna never again put up a Christmas tree. Most of their neighbors in Skokie were Jewish and many were Holocaust survivors. When their two sons started school, Erna joined the PTA and, after a few years, she was elected PTA president. Now she was really "American." Fiercely patriotic, admiring President Eisenhower, she became a committed Republican. She loved expressing her strong views, getting to know "important" people, and soon she was involved in Skokie politics.

In the meantime, five years after Erna and Henry moved to Skokie, Nathan and Riva also bought a home in Skokie. They had a daughter and a son. Nathan developed a successful painting business. Nathan was gregarious and loved to have people around him. There was always noise in their household.

It took my parents eight more years, but they, too, moved to Skokie, buying a two-family house, living in the downstairs apartment, tenants upstairs. By that time, I had married and was living in New York.

And, by that time, my family seemed "normal." They no longer worried about food. They dressed nicely. They laughed. Sometimes. They didn't talk about the war.

Then it changed. Headlines in the *New York Times*: "Neo-Nazis Plan March in Skokie."

My mother telephoned that night.

"Those Nazis want to march here!"

"We won't let them," my father on the extension, his voice tight. "It can't happen here."

In 1977, neo-Nazis announced their intention to demonstrate in Skokie, Illinois. Legal battles followed. Lawyers for the Village obtained a court injunction to block the demonstration. When that was not upheld, the Anti-Defamation League, on behalf of survivors, went to court for a second injunction. The Village Council passed ordinances against the demonstration; these were challenged in other courts by the American Civil Liberties Union. The publicity over the neo-Nazi intent and the lawsuits to stop the march became a national issue: the Constitutional right of free speech—did it extend to the right of the neo-Nazis, with their doctrine of racial superiority and death to Jews and others, to march in front of the homes of those whose families had been exterminated by Nazis? People came to demonstrate from all over the country, some to oppose the march, some to support it.

Erna was among the first, and one of the most vocal, opponents of the Nazi's right to march. As the lawyers made their arguments in court, Erna and other survivors made their arguments in the public forum. Erna, already a seasoned politician, organized in the community. This woman who once hid behind a Christmas tree told people she was a Jew and a survivor. Her story appeared in newspapers across the country. She would not be intimidated. She gave speeches, brought pressure on local politicians, and worked with the Skokie mayor, Albert Smith.

The court cases went on for more than a year. The Village of Skokie and the survivors lost their attempt to prevent the Nazi march in Skokie. Ultimately, the neo-Nazis did not march in Skokie, despite their legal victories. They took their demonstration to Chicago's Marquette Park instead.

The survivors lost the legal battles, but they won, nevertheless. Because of the battle, many of them, though sadly not my parents, felt free to speak, to remember. They had a mission now, to tell the world, to educate, to speak against intolerance, to prevent another Holocaust.

Erna became a voice of American Holocaust survivors. She founded the Holocaust Memorial Foundation of Illinois, which became a prototype for similar foundations in other states. Tirelessly, she lobbied the Illinois State Legislature until Illinois became the first state in the union to pass a law requiring that the Holocaust be taught in the Illinois public schools.

"Education is the key," Erna emphasized. "I want young people to learn from the memory of the Holocaust and keep it from happening again." The legislation she worked for has been followed in other states. In 1987, President Reagan appointed Erna to the United States Holocaust Memorial Council, the organization that saw to the construction of the Holocaust Memorial Museum in Washington, DC.

But they all left Skokie. Nathan and Riva moved to Florida within the year. My mother and father followed, and Erna and Henry moved to another community in Illinois.

The fog comes
on little cat feet.

It sits looking
over harbor and city
on silent haunches
and then moves on.

"Fog," by Carl Sandburg

29

My Mother—After

"OOPS, WHERE ARE MY glasses?" my husband asked. He was sitting in the small TV room in our home, reading the newspaper. He'd arrived at the age where he took his glasses off to read and left them wherever he happened to be.

"Wherever you were when you took them off," I replied.

Richard jumped up, searched on the table, under the table, on the couch, under the newspapers. Then he was out of the study, down the hall, into the bedroom, searching every surface and drawer.

"If you would just put your glasses in the same place, you wouldn't lose them," I said irritably.

I picked myself up and slouched into the kitchen, desultorily looking in places where I'd found his glasses before. They were not on top of the refrigerator or next to the coffeepot.

Richard ran down the stairs, now going to his study.

"What about the garage?" I shouted after him as I walked toward the living room. Then I stopped. "I can't stand this." My voice continued to rise. "I'm not wasting any more time looking for your glasses."

The words were familiar. Standing in the hall of my modern house, I was transported to our apartment in Chicago. My mother had lost her glasses. She lost everything: keys, glasses, wallet. My father dropped what he was doing to help her look. I was supposed to help too, but I was angry. Why did she lose things? Why couldn't she do anything right?

I was nine when my mother came home from the hospital for good. My father had to teach her to dress herself, clean house, shop; and he had to teach her to cook.

The first thing my mother relearned to cook was chicken soup. She'd put water in a pot, add the chicken, cut up carrots, onions, and celery, turn on the flame, and cover the pot. Then she'd sit and patiently wait for the soup to cook.

My mother served chicken soup again and again and again. After a while, I couldn't stand the moist smell of the soup, the soft blandness of the chicken, the overcooked vegetables. But unable to cook anything else and unwilling to discard any food after the hungry years, my mother would continue cooking chicken soup and eating some each day, until all the leftover chicken soup, the stewed chicken, the vegetables, were gone. She was gaining weight.

After a while, she learned other dishes. Her hands were raw and red as she worked in the kitchen, chopping fish, slicing carrots, sautéing onions, forming gefilte fish, rolling matzoh balls, making kreplach. Since she didn't have her mother's recipes, she studied *The Art of Jewish Cooking* by Jennie Grossinger and learned to make our traditional foods.

My mother refused to talk about her "illness." My father feared any talk about the war would bring about a relapse. So we banished talk about the past.

My mother tried to be "normal." She went to school and learned English. She studied American history and government and got her citizenship papers. She tried.

Here's an imaginary photograph:

The left side is dark and crumpled, as if someone tried to destroy it; its edges are damaged and charred. In contrast, the right side of the photograph looks undamaged, untouched, clear and bright and washed in sunlight. My husband and children stand at the right. Just left of center stands my father, looking straight at the camera through dark rimmed glasses. He's about forty-five, wearing a short-sleeved shirt and brown trousers. He's compact, muscular, five foot nine, and, oh, he's not the tallest man in the world, as I thought when I was small. My two uncles, my mother's brothers, stand at the left of the photograph, separated from my father by a small space.

My mother is in the background of this imaginary photograph, in the shadows, behind thick trees and leaves. Looking carefully, I see glimpses of her, pieces of her, an ear or an eye, or her forehead. Try as I might, I cannot see all of her.

In the imaginary photograph in my mind, I stand in the center, where the dark and light meet.

30

❦

My Father—After

M Y FATHER'S SHOES WERE speckled with paint.
    "Look, Ma," my daughter Randi shouted, pointing up the tree.

I shielded my eyes as I looked to where my father had climbed.

My father was seventy-six years old. It was the summer of 1988. My father and mother had come for a visit from Florida, where they lived, to the suburban home in New York where I lived with my husband, Richard, and our two daughters, Randi and Debbie. On the last day of my parents' visit, we sat in the living room, rehashing the events of the past two weeks. It was a windy day, and as we talked, we heard thumping and scratching on the roof of our house. We lived in a redwood contemporary, no attic, and outside sounds came through clearly, an effect Richard and I loved because it brought us closer to nature.

"What's that?" my father asked, instantly alert. He stood to look out the window.

"Oh, it's just that old tree. We'll have to get someone to come and cut it back."

"Why spend the money? I can do it."

"But you're leaving tomorrow."

"That's nothing. We're driving. We can leave a day later."

The next morning, before anyone had woken, my father went to the hardware store and bought a small handsaw. Still drowsy, I heard noises in the backyard. I got up and looked out my bedroom window, which faced the old locust tree. There was my father, propping our tallest ladder against the tree.

I pulled on jeans and a shirt and ran out into the backyard. My mother was already there, one hand on her hip, the other shading her eyes, as she kept up a steady commentary.

"Mundek, be careful. Don't fall down. Why are you doing this? Let's hire someone. It's not a job for you. Let's go home. Oh, watch the ladder. Be careful."

I stood next to her. After a while, my husband and daughters joined us in the backyard, looking on as my father climbed easily to the top of the ladder. He was wearing brown leather oxfords, Florsheim's. He never wore anything else.

When we had disembarked from the SS *Marine Tiger* in New York, HIAS gave my father five dollars for the three of us. My mother's family helped us get to Chicago and found us a place to live. After that, my father looked for work.

"My English wasn't good enough for office work. I didn't know what I would do," he later told me. For a few months, he worked as a salesman in a fabric store frequented by Polish and Jewish immigrants. Then my father found a job selling shoes.

"Chicago had two hundred thousand Poles," my father explained. "I got a job in the Polish section. I sold shoes. I was safe. The family was safe."

During those first years, my father worked long hours. Afterward, we'd sit at the dining room table as he helped me with my homework.

For one homework assignment, I had to collect and categorize the leaves of various trees that grew in our Chicago neighborhood. I brought home as many flat green specimens as I could find and spread them out on the dining room table. My father helped me pour through the books I had brought home from the library, matching the shapes and angles of the leaves to the pictures in the books, and helped me draw and paint my own pictures and bind them into a report to bring to school. I learned about the small jagged leaves of the shady maple, the larger leaves of the majestic oak, the fan-shaped leaves of the exotic ginkgo, the clusters of small oval leaves of the honey locust, and the clusters of larger oval leaves and long black seeds that look like dried-out banana peels of the black locust tree.

In our backyard in 1988, my father was climbing a black locust tree. He was wearing overalls speckled with paint, left over from the work he took up after he stopped selling shoes. He sold shoes for five years, the years when my mother became ill, was institutionalized, and came home to begin her recovery. Years later, my father told me that, while my mother was ill, he did not think about what kind of work he was doing or how much money he was earning—just how to get through the day. When she began to recover, he left his job as a shoe salesman to paint houses and try to earn more money. Though he helped me with my homework, for himself he had no patience for study or the law—and no one to support us even if he did.

My father's first week as a painter, I waited at the front door, as usual, to greet him. He came home, covered from top to bottom with paint. Instead of his usual smile and hug, though, he just said, "Please let me by," and walked right past me. I was surprised and confused, worried he was sick. Later, he told me that his muscles ached so badly, he just had to lie down.

After a few months my father was back to his old self. After work, he'd clean himself meticulously and change his clothes; but the acrid turpentine didn't reach all the cracks in his hands, so they remained an unnatural white. His hands reflected him: outwardly hard and calloused, their touch was sensitive and gentle as they removed my splinters or soothed my hurts, both real and imagined. He would wash and comb my hair, taking care to hold each strand as he combed so the knots he was untangling wouldn't pull and hurt.

His shoes, too, reflected him. They were intended to be worn with a suit and tie in a white collar world, just as my father had intended to be a lawyer, in a suit and tie, in a white collar world. Instead, both the shoes and my father worked in jobs available to him. He found comfort in the hard work. "Doesn't leave time to think," he told me.

Outwardly, my father always maintained his good humor. He developed a loyal group of customers with whom he had a good rapport. Sometimes, out on errands, my father and I would run into one of his customers. "How nice to see you," one might say. "So this is the daughter you told me about." And I would beam with pride.

In our backyard in 1988, my father sawed away at the offending branches of the locust tree. I heard the methodical back and forth of the handsaw, a humming sound, a tune.

He loved music: classical music, show tunes, popular songs, he liked them all. Shortly after we came to America, my father bought a record player. He would sing along with the records, then walk around the apartment singing and humming his latest favorite tune. He particularly loved the operetta *The Student Prince* and sang the Latin "Gaudeamus Igitur" or the boisterous drinking song "Drink, Drink, Drink."

In the mornings, as my father shaved, he would sing his old college songs. He might start with a raucous courting song:

Marysiu buzi daj, Mamusi nie pytaj
Bo mamcia tak robiła gdy jeszcze panną była...
Dear Mary, give me a kiss, don't ask your mother
Because your mother did the same when she was a young
    lady....

"Mundek!" my mother would protest, with a pointed look at me. He'd switch to a song that sounded like students making fun of their professor:

Ósma już godzina, lekcja się zaczyna
Belfer do tablicy studęcine wzywa
Heju heju hy belfer rybcie juhy

A studenti zuchy są...
Eight o'clock already, the lesson begins
The professor calls a student to the blackboard
Hey, hey, silly professor
And students are clever...

"Mundek!" my mother called up to my father in the tree, telling him to be careful. Shielding my eyes from the sun, I watched my father's strong arm move back and forth, sawing yet another branch. When I was a little girl, sometimes my father would flex his forearm and bend to show me the large muscle. "Squeeze," he'd say. To my small hands those muscles felt as hard as rocks.

I went into the house and got my camera. I looked up into the leaves, trying to capture my father's face against the blue of the sky. He looked down at me.

"Hi, doll," he called. "See me? I'm on top of the world."

"Perhaps to recall what you did, or what was done, is to remember another person, in another existence. And to choose forgetfulness is to choose life."

Colin Thubron, *Shadow of the Silk Road*, page 58

31

Return to Kazakhstan

M Y FAMILY'S EXPERIENCE WAS an important part of who I am. But whenever I answered a question about myself, I gave the answer my family had carefully crafted: "I was born in Jasło, Poland." And every time I gave that answer, I became someone other than myself.

At thirteen, I browsed *Hammond World Atlas* for hours, searching for clues to the mysterious and faraway place that was my secret past. The map of the Soviet Union took up the entire centerfold of the atlas. I studied the map of browns and greens and blues, delineating elevation, rivers, lakes; my fingers traced the borders of Central Asian Republics. Sounding out odd place names, I found the biggest of the Republics, Kazakhstan. I pressed my nose to the page, carefully studying the map inch by inch, my gaze dropping to the southernmost tip and a little dot, Dzhambul. It exists, I thought, and this fact gave substance to my existence, too. What is it like? I wondered. But the map held no clue.

"Don't think about it," my mother warned. "Don't ever try to go there. They'll keep you."

"Forget," my father said. "We had a hard life. You're American now. You're okay. That's what matters."

So I forgot. I grew up. I had children of my own. Sadly, my mother, then my father, died. The Soviet Union fell. The Central Asian Republics, Kazakhstan among them, declared their independence. Travel there became easier.

"Go with me," I asked cousin Oskar, ten years older than me. "You'll remember. You'll help me find everything." But he said no. "It's dangerous, unstable." And I realized he was not able to forget.

And then, one day, I met Mira, a lively woman with a round face framed by short black hair.

"Meiramkul is my Kazakh name," she told me, in a thick accent that hinted of Kazakh and Russian.

"When did you come to the US?" I asked.

"Six years ago."

"From Almaty?"

"Mmm, I went to university there. I'm from Dzhambul."

"What?" I gasped. "There's really a Dzhambul?" Excitedly, I asked question after question, and, before we parted, I promised her—and myself—that we would go there together.

The following year, four of us took the journey: my husband Richard, supportive and positive, with none of the emotional baggage I carry; Mira, excited to be visiting her family again; Mira's daughter, Aika, nineteen, tall, and charming with a magnetic smile and soft Asian features; and me, struggling to recover childhood memories.

On our Lufthansa flight to Frankfurt, Mira explained Kazakh history and culture, which she continued to do for the three weeks of our trip. The country was influenced by Russia for a long time. In the nineteenth century, Kazakhstan asked Russia's protection against aggressive invaders and in this way came to be dominated by Russia, first under the czars and then the Communists, until the Soviet Union collapsed in 1991. Most Kazakhs continue to have a strong connection with Russia, even after achieving independence and despite a growing national spirit in Kazakhstan.

"The Kazakh people are direct and ask questions about everything," Mira warned, "so be prepared. One of the first questions you'll be asked is 'How much do you earn.'"

Mira was incensed about a recent TV show in the US where it was said Kazakhs marry their cousins. "Nothing is further from the truth! The person interviewed on that TV show who made such an incorrect statement was, in fact, an Uzbek! Kazakhs have a serious rule against intermarriage. The rule of seven applies. Each person knows his or her family tree up at least seven levels and knows every relative from that point down; one cannot marry within that circle."

Her patter continued as we changed planes in Frankfurt, and I heard the pilot announce our destination, "Almaty." I could not believe I was actually on the way, thinking of the careful way my family shared their true history, in hushed tones, only among those of us who were there. When my uncle Nathan, in his careless, exuberant way, said to an outsider, "See that one?" pointing to me, "Do you know where she was born?" my father's strong gaze stopped him. So, the history felt almost mythical to me.

Traveling to Kazakhstan, I hoped to see something familiar to trigger memories, those stored memories children gather before there is consciousness. I knew I would. I hoped. I imagined—or did I remember?—a dusty house, a fence, two apple trees, a big scary dog; dirt roads, a sooty train station. I searched to rewind the years, to see my father, my mother, as they were then. I longed to reach memories of my mother, miraculously restored, without the prism of her shattered mind.

As I ruminated on the past, Mira's voice brought me back to the present. Her dark hair swinging from side to side, she animatedly told me about her home in Dzhambul: "The city is called Taraz now. Dzhambul was the name of a Communist poet; after Communism fell, the city's ancient name of Taraz was restored."

Our flight landed in Almaty at three a.m. on a dark Sunday morning. The approach, in rain and wind, was bumpy, and I grabbed Richard's arm. "I should have listened to my mother."

I had an overwhelming longing for my daughters in New York. At that moment, the future seemed infinitely more important than any past or secrets. Why was I here? But then the plane jolted to the ground and my anxiety ended.

In a few days, we were in a car with a driver taking us the 450 kilometers to Taraz, eight hours on partly unfinished roads.

"*Jusan,*" Mira said. She leaned out the car window and broke off a twig. "The grass of Kazakhstan. I miss the smell." She held the twig under my nose. I inhaled deeply, but the fresh, minty aroma held no memory for me. My parents didn't talk about the smell of evergreen, or of dry, dusty earth, or of crisp morning breezes that give way to the strong sun of midday in summer. They didn't speak of white apple blossoms in the Kazakhstan spring or red-dotted fields of tulips, or gurgling rivers.

"Do you see train tracks?" I asked, looking for signs that my family might have journeyed this way from the city then called Alma Ata, but Richard shook his head. They would have passed through here about the same time of year, August. My pregnant, starved mother. Was this the beginning? Or was it earlier, in Siberia? Or even earlier?

As we drove west, the modern four-lane highway narrowed, traffic thinned. We saw unpaved lanes, distant huts, sometimes herds of sheep, a few cows, and for a while, nothing, not even dirt roads, just tire tracks imbedded into fields. When our car was forced onto a detour of rutted dirt and gravel, I didn't mind the bouncing and potholes; it felt more authentic to me, focused on my family's struggles. When I was growing up, my parents were fastidious about hygiene and food spoilage, and I could not conjure them on this journey, terrified of being sent back to Siberia, not knowing where they were fleeing to, starved, no bathroom facilities, no water, only the worn clothes on their backs and barely a place to sit. I felt guilty, sitting comfortably in the back of the air-conditioned Honda Civic, Richard beside me, our suitcases full of clothes and gifts, and more snacks for three weeks than my family had in all their years here.

But they survived.

We passed another village, a few ramshackle houses, others neatly painted with blue trim, boys at a card table with hand-lettered signs selling cola, Moslem cemeteries marked by small stone minarets.

Mira talked constantly, her voice getting hoarse, and I was eager to learn all I could. "Kazakhs are pragmatic. Their harsh existence allowed no sentimentality over animals raised for food. They raise beautiful horses, racehorses called *kulan lugovoe*, that some say rival the famed Arabian stallions. But they also raise different breeds of horses for food." We drove past many herds of horses looking like cattle. "In the winter, each family uses one horse." Richard, my American husband, recoiled a bit. Mira didn't notice.

Finally, we entered the outskirts of Taraz to a vista that surprised me. My parents never described purple mountains beneath brilliant blue skies framing the city's edge. Then, at last, I saw train tracks to our left, parallel to the highway, with rusted freight cars.

"You'll see Kazakh hospitality and generosity," Mira continued without pause. Their nomadic lifestyle taught them to honor guests who brought news of the outside world and broke the monotony of life on the steppe. And, true to this tradition, during our weeks there, Kazakhs opened their doors to us and their hearts as well. I met a few others, outsiders like my family, who told how they were given places to live and food even at a time when the Kazakhs themselves were facing harsh deprivations.

In Dzhambul, we connected with the small remnants of the Jewish community. A frail man named Vasily drove us in his ancient blue Moskvitch to the home of ruddy-faced Bronia, a woman of sixty-seven, who lived in a small frame home with a tiny closed-in porch used as a kitchen. Bronia served tea and cookies at an oilcloth-covered table while she told us her story of coming to Dzhambul as a one-and-a-half-year-old orphan in 1941, with an older brother who knew they were Jewish. She attended school in the sugar factory and worked there for fifty years. Bronia removed two small objects from a drawer and proudly held them in her cupped hands: a medal with a red star "for fifty years of service," and another red enamel medal "for good work."

Looking at those medals, I thought of what might have been and was overwhelmed with gratitude to my mother, father, and uncles, for their courage and tenacity, for their love, for my luck, for getting out.

We met others and heard similar stories. One person told us: "The Kazakhs discriminate against each other, the different tribes, but Kazakhs never discriminated against Jews." Mira swelled with pride.

I asked everyone I met, professors, historians, even a jurist Mira knew, about a possible law in Dzhambul under which my family was given the hajaika's house to live in, but no one knew of it. A journalist told us there was, and still is, a law that every citizen of Kazakhstan—which, includes a child born in the country—is entitled to ten *sotkas* of land, about one hundred by one hundred meters. Could this have been the law, translated during the war years, that provided a roof over our heads?

We learned that, in earlier times, Dzhambul had many apple trees, like those in my hajaika's yard. There was a bazaar near the railroad station; maybe that was where my father sold ice cream. There were many small flour mills, and, coincidentally, the main mill was on the site of the Gazovik Hotel where Richard and I stayed. Could that have been where my father and Henek worked? The black market took place on the square in front of the hotel. Is this where Tulek traded?

We heard the twelfth-century legend of Aisha-bibi, a Kazakh Romeo and Juliet story, and visited two monuments constructed for the doomed lovers, but these held no resonance for me. We were stopped at a police checkpoint and asked for our passports and registrations, but I did not feel threatened by the demeanor of the police, with their round hats pushed to the back of their heads like halos.

One day, Mira's brother-in-law Quandak, a doctor, drove us to visit the Railroad Hospital, across the street from the train station. This was a maternity hospital during the war years and for a very long time, he explained. I walked through the complex of white brick buildings, some dilapidated and in disrepair, others less so and still in use, and wondered if this was where I was born. I imagined my family: starved, scared, fugitive, penniless; my mother, terrified, in pain, screaming.

"Records are no longer available," the head doctor, a Korean woman, told us. "The hospital was free. It admitted everyone, asked no documentation, refused no refugee." She was born in 1938, she told us, and her family, fleeing Chinese aggression, somehow got to Dzhambul, where the people helped them and took them in.

"A remarkably giving people," she said.

Quandak drove us to the former Railroad Institute where David and Selma lived in an orphanage and school; it had been turned into a police station.

As we drove or walked around the city, I looked at every house and asked if it could have been my home for more than three years. Arochoks lined most city streets, and as we passed those and saw the swift rushing waters of the Karasum River, I wondered where my mother washed laundry and where she feared I fell in.

Quandak took us to the train station. I was startled to realize that this was a major hub; there were at least ten tracks across and many sidings holding faded freight trains or rusted flatbeds. A footbridge crossed this massive expanse. Is this the station where my family arrived so many years ago, I wondered? Could this be the footbridge my father crossed at four a.m. when he bought ice to make ice cream?

Another day, I searched for the newspaper where Henek worked for a time. In the city's main square, I saw a sign for a paper, *Znamya Truda*, "In the Name of Truth." Upstairs sat a woman in a white lace skirt and blouse behind a stylish desk in an office decorated with old newspapers. This used to be called the *Dzhambul Communist*, she told us, and there were old records and photos. But there would be no photos or records of workers like Henek, a typesetter; only records of important people.

We continued to search for the hajaika's house, helped by Mira's background in this city and the many officials she had worked with. "Here everything depends on who you know," she said. "You do something for someone and then he owes you a favor back."

We went to the office of the chief of archives, to the land records office, then to yet another office where old records of addresses were kept, to a "center for helping people" where we were asked if there was anything like that in the United States. Days passed as we searched for, found, and scrutinized records of people with the surnames of Rieger, Gans, and the hajaika's name, Peredereyeva, if Oskar was even right about that name. But we found no evidence of my family. They had achieved their goal; there were no records that they—that I—had been in Dzhambul.

At last, somebody directed us to the *zaks*, the birth registry, in the main square near our hotel. After much bureaucratic wrangling, we found a fashionably dressed woman behind a desk who gave authorization for an archivist to look for my birth records.

In another office, a lady archivist pulled out a bound ledger, about four inches by six inches, flipped the pages, and there it was! A document, partly printed, partly handwritten, recited the birth of Anna Rieger on October 18. The birth was registered on November 1. The paper gave my father's name, Mojses Rieger, age twenty-nine, and occupation, "temporarily unemployed." My mother was twenty-seven and a housewife. Their address, where they'd been since October 12, was Technichna 51. The birth registry was signed by my father. His handwriting looked odd to me, until I realized he was uncertain with the Russian alphabet.

I asked for a copy of my birth certificate. The archivist said the birth certificate, number 121336, was given to my parents. Huh? Did they have it? Did they lose it? Destroy it? I remember their lifelong fear that I'd be kept by, or taken by, or returned to, the Soviets.

Ah, but I could request a duplicate, the archivist explained, if I brought a translated and notarized copy of my US passport, an official letter requesting a copy of this record, certain other documentation, and 1,292 *tenge*.

During the many days it took to arrange this documentation, I focused on the address, Technichna 51. That couldn't be the hajaika's house, I thought, because we were given her home only as a result of my birth, I was told. My father probably registered my birth, the only time he came to the authorities, to make me eligible for the housing. Technichna 51 must have been only a temporary shelter. Somebody told us the street name had changed, it was now Permanova, but the numbers were the same.

The footbridge crossing the railroad tracks led directly to the street. Number 51 was only a short walk from the bridge. The white adobe house was encircled by a blue, corrugated fence.

We entered the gate and rang the doorbell. Natasha, a pretty woman, thirty-three years old, invited us to come in. The house was built before the war, she explained. It had two rooms and an enclosed porch; three other rooms were added later. I studied the small rooms. Could these have held all of us, my mother, father, Henek, me, a stove and a table; Tulek and Oskar on the porch; and the hajaika in rooms of her own? The backyard was narrow and deep with an outhouse, a small shed, a well with a hand pump. I imagined a bigger house, a bigger yard facing the street. Still...I looked at Richard. Could be, I said slowly.

Inside, Natasha showed us a yellowed register with names of owners of the house, and those who roomed here, about forty in all, but the oldest date was 1973. Natasha sent us to a next-door neighbor who might know, a white-haired woman born in 1941. This other woman told us that, for as long as she could remember, the house belonged to people named Gorshin and there were no temporary borders. Did she have a childhood friend named Anna? She shook her head. Did her family ever talk about a family who left suddenly? Again she shook her head.

I was at the end of my quest.

We returned to the Zaks with documentation and money, and at last obtained a copy of my birth record. The next day, we flew home. I was relaxed, my mission more than complete. I hadn't reclaimed lost memories of my infancy. I hadn't found the house where I lived—or had I? But I had a birth record, an image of modern Taraz, a profound respect for the determination of my family, and a newfound knowledge of the kindness of people living in a different culture halfway around the globe.

"*Zimlechka,*" Mira calls me, the Russian word for countryman. "It's *jirles* in Kazakh." "Like *landsman* in Yiddish," Richard comments. I am all of these and more. I located roots in Poland and Kazakhstan, uncovered family history in the Soviet Union, Germany, and France; but I found my home in the United States.

Yes. I am an American girl.

I will arise and go now, and go to Innisfree,
And a small cabin build there, of clay and wattles made;
Nine bean-rows will I have there, a hive for the honey
    bee,
And live alone in the bee-loud glade.

And I shall have some peace there, for peace comes
    dropping slow,
Dropping from the veils of the morning to where the
    cricket sings;
There midnight's all a glimmer, and noon a purple glow,
And evening full of the linnet's wings.

I will arise and go now, for always night and day
I hear lake water lapping with low sounds by the shore;
While I stand on the roadway, or on the pavements
    gray,
I hear it in the deep heart's core.

"The Lake Isle of Innisfree," by
William Butler Yeats

There is so much to say. One thing.... No more war. Peace. Why are people killing people? People are all the same. I went through half the world. They're all the same. Nobody's different. Even if they speak different languages, they are the same, they eat the same, they live the same, they walk the same. Why is it that people are killing one another?

Be friendly, make peace with one another. Why fight? We are human beings, we should be friends, people should not have to suffer the way we did. There is no reason for it.

The world can live as one big world. There is plenty of room and earth and ground for everybody. Don't fight, be peaceful, enjoy life.

Murray (Mundek) Rieger
Interview by USC Shoah Foundation
Institute for Visual History and Education,
University of Southern California
Hallandale, Florida, USA
November 14, 1995
Tape 8674
(Herein "Shoah video")

Acknowledgments

THIS WORK COULD NOT have been written without the help and enthusiasm of many. Mira Ness taught me about the giving people of Kazakhstan, showed me the country, and shared her warm and extensive family. Joanna Morgan spent countless hours at my kitchen table translating my father's letters from Polish and other documents from Russian. Veronica Golos was the first to give me the courage to write, and Susan Wenger was invaluable in editing and shaping the final version. Friends Margaret and John Sheehan believed there would be interest in my story, while Rita and Eitan Raz and Sandi and Sam Duboff listened to countless narratives as I found my writing voice. Joe Gans, Helen Siewierski, Yetta and Sam Rosenberg, David Gans, and others shared their memories. Alan Gans, Ira Gans, Michel Rieger, Francois Rieger, Aude Rieger, and Claire Rieger remembered family stories. Countless others expressed interest and kept me going with their enthusiasm. My daughters, Randi Wender and Deborah Hoffman, the lights of my life, were integrally involved, and even more so was my ever-supportive husband, Richard, who was with me every step of the way as I recovered childhood memories.

Made in the USA
Middletown, DE
02 May 2015